THE CANADA-U.S. CAPITAL MARKET: INTERMEDIATION, INTEGRATION, AND POLICY INDEPENDENCE

Robert M. Dunn, Jr.
George Washington University

CANADA-U.S. PROSPECTS
a series sponsored by
C. D. Howe Research Institute (Canada)
National Planning Association (U.S.A.)

79-840
Legal Deposit — 4th Quarter 1978
Quebec National Library
Library of Congress Catalogue Number 78-71657
ISBN 0-88806-046-7
November, 1978, $6.00
Quotation with appropriate credit is permissible
C. D. Howe Research Institute (Montreal, Quebec) and
National Planning Association (Washington, D.C.)
Printed in Canada

CONTENTS

iii

Appendix A: Tables

Appendix B: North American Financial Integration Questionnaire

Tables

Charts

Figure

FOREWORD

Financial transactions amounting to many billions of dollars take place each year across the Canada-U.S. border. These transactions provide one very concrete example of what is meant by the observation that the two economies have become highly integrated.

Over the years Canada has been a large net importer of financial capital from the United States, giving rise to massive debt liabilities and substantial U.S. ownership claims on production facilities located in Canada. As a result, Canadians have become increasingly concerned about their country's growing indebtedness to the United States, although prolonged debate on how to relieve this situation has produced little effective action.

While commentaries on the bilateral financial relationship tend to concentrate on net inflows of capital into Canada, these net inflows are the outcome of much larger flows moving in both directions across the border. These two-way flows reflect the fact that the United States serves what are referred to as financial intermediary functions for Canada, matching lenders' objectives and borrowers' needs in an effective and efficient manner. Canadian financial institutions have been increasing their capacities to carry on these functions, but relatively free movement of funds across the border continues to benefit both countries.

This study examines both gross and net bilateral financial transactions. Using responses from members of the Canadian-American Committee to a questionnaire circulated by the author, it analyzes many of the main reasons why these transactions occur. Some of the major issues raised concerning the Canada-U.S. financial relationship are also analyzed, and the author reviews the theory of, and experience with, flexible exchange rates as a means whereby Canada might obtain greater policy independence in financial matters from the United States.

The author of this study, Robert M. Dunn, Jr., is Professor of Economics at George Washington University in Washington, D.C. His numerous publications include *Canada's Experience with Fixed and Flexible Exchange Rates in a North American Capital Market*, which was released by the Canadian-American Committee in 1971.

This study analyzes bilateral financial developments prior to 1978. The period since then has witnessed some highly disruptive pressures in the North American capital market; these more recent developments will be examined in the concluding study of the Canada-U.S. Prospects series.

Carl E. Beigie
Series Coordinator

PREFACE

This study began in the fall of 1975, at a time when Canadian-U.S. relations were somewhat more strained than usual. The research undertaken for it was designed in part to deal with the financial aspects of these strains. During the past three years, relations between the two countries have improved considerably, and the focus of this study has been shifted slightly to reflect that development. Its underlying theme, however, has not been changed. The extent to which the Canadian economy and society are integrated, or entangled, with those of the United States will always be a major issue in Canadian life; this study deals with the financial aspects of that integration.

Research for this study could not have been completed without the aid of many people and organizations. The members of the Canadian-American Committee were particularly helpful in answering a rather long and detailed questionnaire and in providing access to members of the two countries' financial communities, who were also willing to provide replies. The following individuals and institutions answered the questionnaire; without their efforts and expertise, this project could not have been completed.

John Chant of Carleton University
Peter Martin of McLeod, Young & Weir
Jack Popkin of Pitfield Mackay Ross Limited
Richard Wurzel of A. E. Ames & Co. Limited

L'Assurance-Vie Desjardins
Avco Financial Services Canada Limited
Avco Financial Services, Inc. (United States)
Banque Canadienne Nationale
Bank of Canada
Bank of Montreal
The Bank of Nova Scotia
Canadian Imperial Bank of Commerce
Canada Permanent Trust Company
The Chase Manhattan Bank
Citicorp
Greenshields Incorporated
Hydro-Québec
Metropolitan Life Insurance Company
Ministry of Finance, Ottawa
The Morgan Trust Company
The Provincial Bank of Canada
The Royal Bank of Canada
The Royal Trust Company Mortgage Corporation
Salomon Brothers

Sun Life Assurance Company of Canada
Wood Gundy Limited

The staffs of the C. D. Howe Research Institute and the National Planning Association were also very helpful in this effort. Carl Beigie carried the primary advisory and editorial responsibility and deserves particular thanks. Prompt and accurate typing was provided by Nancy Roberts. I wish especially to thank Bohn Young Koo for assistance in the preparation of statistical material for this study. Finally, the financial assistance of the foundations supporting the project of which this study is a part is gratefully acknowledged.

1

Introduction and Summary

The degree of economic and financial integration existing between Canada and the United States is probably as great as for any other two independent countries in the world. The extent of this integration is far more apparent to Canadians than to residents of the United States, however, and consequently is more controversial in Canada. The question of whether the potentially sizable economic benefits of close ties with the United States justify both the real and the imagined costs in terms of lost or compromised national independence has been a major theme in Canadian politics since Confederation. This issue was a dominant one on the Canadian political scene in the early 1970s, but has declined in importance in recent years as Quebec separatism, inflation, and unemployment became more serious immediate concerns. However, it is quite likely that, as these current problems are solved or become less serious, Canadian writers and political leaders will return to their previous debate over the advantages and disadvantages of their country's close economic and financial ties with the United States.

This study is one of a series, each volume of which deals in some detail with various important, or at least controversial, aspects of the Canadian-U.S. relationship. The purpose of this study is to analyze the relationship between the capital markets of Canada and the United States during the past decade or so, with particular emphasis on factors producing two-directional capital flows across the border. When short-term capital flows in one direction and long-term funds flow in the opposite direction, as is typically the case in the Canadian-U.S. experience, the capital markets and financial institutions of one country are acting as financial intermediaries between savers and borrowers in the other.

Financial intermediaries exist because savers typically want to hold assets that are relatively liquid and that do not involve large risks, whereas most borrowers are less than perfect risks and want funds for long periods of time. Financial intermediaries, such as banks or mutual funds, exist in order to bridge this gap between the type of assets that savers want to hold and those that borrowers want to issue. Intermediaries perform this bridge function by issuing

1

relatively liquid claims, such as bank deposits or mutual-fund shares, and using the funds thus acquired to purchase less liquid assets, such as long-term notes or common stocks. The intermediary's income results from the fact that the yield is usually higher on long-term, and hence risky, assets than on the short-term assets that the intermediary issues to the public. The intermediary can afford to hold a relatively illiquid portfolio on the basis of more liquid liabilities because it can assume that maturing liabilities will be replaced or rolled over. In the case of banks, this ability to maintain a balance sheet on which the assets are less liquid than the liabilities is enhanced by the existence of a central bank acting as a lender of last resort if heavy withdrawals take place.

Financial intermediation can occur within an economy or between economies, and one of the main purposes of this study is to explain why the historic pattern of intermediation between Canada and the United States, in which short-term funds flow to New York and long-term funds return to Canada, has developed.

The effect of the introduction of flexible exchange rates on the pattern of capital flows between the two countries and the resulting impact of floating rates on the independence and effectiveness of Canadian economic policies are elements of a second area that will receive some attention.

A third area of emphasis includes the factors that have produced large and continuing net flows of capital to Canada despite an advanced level of economic development there, with resulting high per capita incomes that would seem to make such continuing capital inflows unnecessary. Most economies import capital during the early and middle stages of economic growth but reverse this flow later in the development process and become net capital exporters. Canada appears to be an exception to this pattern, and one purpose of this study is to suggest why this has been the case and what might be done to reduce or eliminate Canada's dependence on net capital inflows if such a change were to become a Canadian policy goal.

It is not suggested that greater capital self-sufficiency necessarily ought to be a Canadian goal, but if the federal government maintains a policy objective of making the country less dependent on the United States, a reduction in the extent to which Canada requires large inflows of foreign capital — the vast majority of which has come from the United States — would appear to be an obvious priority. It is equally possible, however, that Canadians will ultimately decide that the goal of making their country more independent of the United States does not justify the type of policies that would be necessary to reduce or eliminate Canada's reliance on large net flows of capital from that country. One aim of this study is to suggest what these policies might be, which requires an understanding of why Canada continues to attract, and to depend on, these inflows. Whatever Canadian voters and their elected government finally decide on this issue, it should be useful at least to understand why the past and current pattern of capital inflows exists and what policies would be required to change it.

Theoretical Framework

The theory of international capital flows and of financial intermediation is covered in Chapter 2. Although the chapter does not relate specifically to the Canadian-U.S. case, it does emphasize those parts of the existing theory that are particularly relevant to the relationship between the Canadian and U.S. capital markets. It deals first with the forces producing continuing net flows of capital from one country to another, the most important of which are differences in the capital/labor (or capital/land) ratios of the two countries. Capital will typically flow from countries where the capital/labor (or capital/land) ratio is relatively high to countries where the ratio is relatively low. Where capital is abundant relative to other factors of production, it has a relatively low yield, and vice versa. Capital flows respond to these differences in relative scarcities and yields and have the effect over time of reducing them. Canada's natural resource base means a low capital/land ratio, which attracts capital. The high rate of Canadian immigration has caused a particularly rapid expansion of the labor force, which reduces the capital/labor ratio, which also serves to attract capital to Canada.

Chapter 2 then deals with the causes of two-directional capital flows, or international financial intermediation, at somewhat greater length. Although there is no single cause of such patterns of capital flows, the most important argument relates to differing yield structures in the two countries. A yield curve describes the relationship among interest rates for differing maturities; the curve rises if long-term interest rates are higher than short-term interest rates, and vice versa. Rising yield curves are the norm in any country because of the lower liquidity and greater risk that result from holding long-term assets, but the steepness of yield curves may vary significantly from one country to another. If Canada's yield curve is steeper than that prevailing in the United States, as has typically been the case, the greater margin between Canadian long-term and short-term yields encourages a two-directional flow of capital between Canadian and U.S. capital markets. Short-term funds flow from Toronto to New York, and long-term capital flows in the opposite direction. Since the basic role of a financial intermediary is to borrow short-term funds and to lend long-term funds, this situation implies that New York is acting as a financial intermediary for the Canadian economy.

If international financial intermediation occurs primarily because the steepness of yield curves differs significantly among countries, the next question is why such yield-curve differences exist. In terms of this study, the question becomes why the Canadian yield curve is almost always steeper than that prevailing in New York. There are a number of forces capable of producing this result, including differences in the degree of liquidity preference in the two countries. If Canadian savers and portfolio managers have a particularly strong desire to hold short-term, and hence highly liquid, assets and if this desire is much less strong in the United States, Canada will tend to have a steeper yield curve than will the United States. Differences in the competitiveness and efficiency of the capital markets of the two countries can produce the same result. Low-cost and highly competitive capital markets will tend to cause somewhat flatter yield curves. For quite different reasons, capital markets that are relatively small, illiquid, or unstable will encourage steeper yield curves. Finally, the steepness of a yield curve may reflect in part the nature of the industries that are the dominant borrowers in that capital market. If the rapidly growing sectors of an economy are manufacturing and resource-based industries requiring large amounts of long-term capital, the result will be a particularly heavy demand for funds at the long end of the market and a steeper yield curve as bond yields rise to allocate the available long-term funds. If, however, the dominant borrowers need short-term funds, the result will be far less pressure on bond markets and a flatter yield curve.

Chapter 2 also deals with the effects of international capital flows on the internal economy. Large net flows of capital have significant income-distribution effects, which explains why various groups may either support or oppose the free movement of capital. Large capital inflows increase the capital/labor and the capital/land ratios and hence increase the return to labor and land, while capital outflows have the opposite effects, which may explain in part why the AFL-CIO would like to restrict outflows of U.S. capital.

The international integration of national capital markets also has significant effects on the independence and effectiveness of domestic monetary policy, the nature of which depends on whether the exchange rate is fixed or flexible. In a world of fixed exchange rates, the existence of international capital flows that are sensitive to relatively small interest-rate differentials greatly limits the independence and influence of national central banks. Flexible exchange rates, however, have the effect of greatly strengthening the independence of domestic monetary policy. Capital flows enhance rather than reduce the effects of monetary-policy shifts on the domestic economy with flexible exchange rates and consequently increase the influence of the central bank. The nature of the exchange-rate regime also has effects on fiscal policy, but these effects are more modest and sometimes uncertain in direction.

Empirical Evidence

Chapters 3 and 4 represent an attempt to interpret the recent relationship between Canadian and U.S. capital markets in terms of the theory presented in Chapter 2. Chapter 3 deals with the relationship primarily in domestic financial and economic terms, while Chapter 4 analyzes the effect of Canada's adoption in 1970 of a flexible exchange rate on that relationship.

Chapter 3 first discusses the extent of Canada's dependence on foreign capital during the post-1950 period. Just over 20 percent of Canada's total net investment during this period has come from foreign resources. This percentage has varied sharply, however, declining from a peak of almost 35 percent in 1955-59 to only 12 percent in 1970-74, before rising sharply in the past three years. This dependence on foreign capital seems very large until it is compared to Canadian GNP rather than to net investment. Total capital inflows during this period represented only about 2-$^{1}/_2$ percent of Canadian GNP, meaning that only a modest increase in its savings rate (private plus public savings) would have made it possible for Canada to maintain historic investment levels without having to rely on foreign resources. A moderate tightening of Canadian fiscal policy, offset by a parallel easing of monetary policy to maintain aggregate demand levels, could have produced this result. The necessary tightening of fiscal policy would not have been easy or popular, but Ottawa could have seen to it that Canada's economy grew as it has without net foreign borrowing.

Recent studies by Thomas Powrie and others attempt to estimate how much economic growth Canada would have lost if foreign capital had been unavailable and if no policy adjustments had been made to increase the Canadian savings rate. A 20 percent reduction in Canadian net investment since 1950 could be expected to have noticeable effects on economic growth, but Powrie concludes that the effects would have been quite small. For a number of reasons, however, Powrie's estimates of these effects appear to be too low; unfortunately, there is no way of knowing the extent of the likely error.

This question of dependence on capital inflows is further complicated when the role of immigration is considered. If Canada had allowed significantly fewer immigrants into the country during the past twenty-five years, the labor force would have grown much less rapidly, and the same level of per capita GNP could have been maintained with significantly less investment, and hence with little or no foreign capital.

Chapter 3 deals primarily with two-directional capital flows between Canada and the United States — that is, with the process of financial intermediation operating between the two countries. The behavior of the Canadian yield curve relative to that prevailing in the United States is a major cause of this intermediation process, and this yield-curve relationship during the past eighteen years is discussed in some detail. Responses to questionnaires sent to a number of capital-market participants in both countries are used to suggest why the yield curve has typically been steeper in Canada than in the United States. Although these responses are inherently speculative and sometimes in conflict, they are highly informed and provide some unusual and perhaps unique insights into the workings of capital markets in the two countries. Although a number of varied and sometimes complicated causes were put forth, the most common single suggestion was that Canadians are inherently more conservative investors and consequently have a strong preference for highly liquid portfolios. This preference increases the demand for short-term paper and reduces that for bonds in Canada, resulting in a steeper yield curve than that found in the United States.

The questionnaire also dealt with forces, other than differences in yields, that encourage capital flows between the two countries. There was strong support for the argument that many large Canadian borrowers go to New York because their financing requirements are so great that Canadian financial institutions cannot prudently fill their needs, irrespective of yield. Projects such as Churchill Falls and James Bay can be financed only in massive capital markets — that is, in New York or London. It was also suggested that relatively unseasoned or high-risk Canadian borrowers have often gone to New York because U.S. banks have simply been less risk-averse than their Canadian counterparts. However, a number of respondents indicated that the difference between the attitudes toward risk in Canadian and in U.S. banks was declining, in part because the unhappy loss experience of many New York banks during recent years has made them more appreciative of the Canadian approach to lending.

Although there are differences between the performances of financial institutions in the two countries and although Canadian banks certainly do face a less demanding competitive climate than their U.S. counterparts, the available data do not indicate that differences in competition and efficiency are a major factor in determining the pattern of capital flows between the two countries. There are, however, a number of instances in which the regulatory policies of the two governments provide strong incentives for capital flows. To a considerable degree, for example, U.S.-dollar banking in Canada and the activities of Canadian banks' agencies in New York have been encouraged, if not caused, by Regulation Q. This regulation strictly limits the interest rates U.S. banks may pay their depositors, but does not affect the behavior of banks in Canada doing business in U.S. dollars or even the operations of the agencies of Canadian banks in New York. The result is a large flow of funds back and forth between New York and Toronto, the major cause of which is Regulation Q.

Exchange-Rate Regimes

Chapter 4 deals primarily with the effects of alternative exchange-rate regimes on capital flows and on other transactions between Canada and the United States. It has been widely argued that flexible exchange rates are undesirable because the additional costs and risks they create for those using the exchange market discourage international trade and capital flows. Despite the frequent repetition of this argument, there is little or no evidence that it is valid for the Canadian experience. It may have had some relevance in the mid-1970s for certain European countries where flexible exchange rates were a totally new system to bankers and traders and where a learning process was necessary before commercial and financial transactions could fully return to their pre-1973 patterns. In Canada, however, the 1950-62 experience with floating rates was more than adequate to familiarize bankers and traders with the system, so that, when Canada adopted a flexible exchange rate again in 1970, the international sector of the economy was merely returning to an environment well-known to Canadian participants. The questionnaire responses supported the conclusion that Canada's adoption of a flexible exchange rate had not discouraged international transactions and suggested a number of methods used to reduce or eliminate exchange risks.

The last part of Chapter 4 contains a discussion of the effects of flexible exchange rates on the management of Canadian monetary and fiscal policies. The results of a number of econometric studies of the Canadian economy are reviewed, all of which reach the conclusion that the effectiveness of Canadian monetary policy was enhanced considerably by the existence of flexible exchange rates in the 1950-62 and post-1970 periods. The effects on fiscal policy are less clear, and it appears that the exchange-rate regime has not had a major impact in this policy area. It is suggested at the end of the chapter, however, that large changes in the exchange rate have such sizable and unpopular effects on various aspects of the Canadian economy that the Bank of Canada and the federal government may be discouraged from adopting otherwise desirable policies that might produce such shifts. The exchange rate can be allowed to float as long as it is fairly stable, but instability in the rate is almost certain to produce policy changes, including exchange-market intervention, that will limit its movement. Despite these difficulties, flexible exchange rates appear to have been a success in Canada and elsewhere, particularly when compared to the crisis-prone parity system of the 1960s.

Policy Options

Chapter 5 deals with some Canadian policy issues raised by the recent pattern of financial relations between the two countries. The

Canadian government indicated in 1971 that it would like the
economy to become less dependent on the United States, although it
now appears that this goal is not regarded with the same urgency in
Ottawa as it was a few years ago.[1] If this goal remains important,
however, it will probably necessitate policies that make Canada less
dependent on foreign capital. As was suggested earlier, it is possible
to shift the mixture of fiscal and monetary policies (tighter fiscal,
easier monetary) in order to produce this result, but the adoption of
such an approach will not be popular or easy. If Canada is serious
about becoming more independent, however, such a policy shift,
along with the continuation of a fairly restrictive immigration policy
to help reduce the rate of growth of the labor force and hence the
need for high levels of investment, deserves serious consideration.
Chapter 5 concludes with a brief discussion of exchange-rate policy
that suggests that, although the recent depreciation of the Canadian
dollar from U.S.103¢ to U.S.89¢ has been disruptive and troublesome, a return to a fixed exchange rate would not be helpful and is
therefore unlikely. At least memories of Canada's difficulties with a
fixed parity in the late 1960s ought to make it unlikely.

---

[1] For the position of the Canadian government at that time, see Mitchell Sharp,
"Canada-U.S. Relations: Options for the Future," *International Perspectives*, Autumn, 1972, pp. 1-24. Mr. Sharp was the Canadian Minister for External Affairs at
the time the article was published.

2

Theoretical Considerations:
Causes and Effects of International Capital Flows

A discussion of the particular relationship between Canadian and U.S. capital markets requires an understanding of the broader context in which international capital flows take place. The purpose of this chapter is to outline briefly the existing theory as to why such flows occur and why fairly extensive integration of separate national capital markets exists. The reasons for *net* flows of capital between countries — that is, flows moving in one direction — are relatively straightforward and will be discussed first. It is less clear why capital ought to flow simultaneously in both directions and in various forms across a border — that is, why a fairly extensive integration of national capital markets ought to develop. That subject will therefore be discussed in somewhat greater length. Finally, the consequences of international financial integration for domestic policy options are reviewed.

Net Flows of Capital

The causes of net flows of capital in one direction begin with differing rates of return — that is, with the obvious point that capital flows from countries where interest rates or profit rates are relatively low to those where they are relatively high. Even that statement, however, must be qualified. If capital were free to move from one country to another and if risks and transactions costs were zero, any significant difference in yields would be "arbitraged" away by movements of funds. One would then observe continuing capital flows even in the absence of major differences in observed interest rates.

The earlier conclusion must then be stated in a more qualified way: net flows of capital occur in response to situations in which significant differences in yields would occur if movements of capital were impossible. Put another way, if capital did flow freely to produce a common interest rate, then the level of investment in one country would exceed the level of savings at that interest rate, with the additional investment's being financed by capital inflows. The reverse would be true in the other country.

This can be clarified by an example. In a two-country world of Canada and the United States, with no capital flows between the two countries, an interest rate of 10 percent might be required in Canada to clear the market for funds — that is, to equate domestic savings and investment — while 6 percent might accomplish the same purpose in the United States. If capital movements then became possible with complete and riskless capital-market integration, capital would flow north, reducing interest rates in Canada and increasing them in the United States. If the arbitraging process were complete, a yield of 7 percent might exist in both capital markets. The decline in interest rates in Canada would increase domestic investment in plant and equipment, and vice versa in the United States. The result would be that, at the new joint interest rate of 7 percent, Canadian investment would exceed domestic savings, with the excess investment's being financed by capital inflows from the United States. In the United States, savings would exceed domestic investment, with the excess funds flowing north. In the real world, however, the existence of exchange-rate and other risks, and of information and transactions costs, means that the arbitraging process can never be complete, so that some yield differentials will always remain despite large capital flows. It remains true, however, that, as a result of actual flows of funds, observed yield differentials between Canada and the United States are considerably narrower than they would be in the absence of capital-market integration.

An important distinction must be made between flows of financial capital and movements of "real" capital — the former representing funds or financial assets, and the latter, real resources such as machinery. The flows of funds from one country to another, as recorded in the capital account of the balance of payments, are not real capital but instead provide financing for the net flows of real resources, as recorded in the current account. Flows of financial capital from the United States to Canada make it possible for Canadian investment to exceed domestic savings by providing financing for a current-account deficit, which in turn provides the necessary real resources for the investment.

If Canadian investment is to exceed domestic savings, the necessary real resources must come from outside the economy, and a current-account deficit is the mechanism through which they are provided. Since the balance of payments accounts must balance, a current-account deficit that provides real capital inflows must be matched by the sum of financial capital inflows, which appear in the capital account, and by any reduction in Canadian foreign-exchange reserves. Net flows of capital into a country can be viewed either as the current-account deficit (real capital) or as the sum of the capital-account and foreign-exchange-reserve items (financial capital), and the two must, by accounting convention, be equal. Attracting financial capital inflows to a country running a current-account deficit is of obvious importance, since foreign-exchange reserves are limited and cannot be run down indefinitely. Beyond the very short run, a country can import real capital through a current-account deficit only to the extent that it attracts the necessary funding through financial capital inflows. Whether capital inflows are measured as a current-account deficit or as a capital-account surplus merely depends on whether the capital is viewed in real or financial terms. If foreign-exchange reserves are constant, the two approaches must lead to the same result.

Causes of Net Capital Flows

To say that capital flows from the United States to Canada in response to differences in yields leads to the question of why such yield differences should exist in the first place, and why they are, in fact, so common. Why is it that at world interest rates the Canadian economy consistently generates insufficient savings to finance domestic investment, while the U.S. economy typically saves more than it invests at the same interest rates?

There are a number of possible answers to this question, the most important being that, other things being equal, returns to capital ought to vary inversely with the ratio of the capital stock to the labor force and with the ratio of the capital stock to the stock of land and other natural resources. Returns to capital ought to be relatively high in countries where the stock of capital is small relative to the supply of labor or land, and vice versa. In each country the relatively scarce factor of production ought to have a high marginal return, and capital should flow from countries where it is relatively abundant to those where it is relatively scarce. For example, the massive amount of land and other natural resources relative to the domestic capital stock in Canada would tend to make the returns to capital high, and vice versa in the United States.

The idea that relative rates of return to capital reflect relative scarcities leads to a view of capital flows that relates to the stages of an economy's development.[1] In the early stages of development a country presumably has a decided scarcity of capital relative to either labor or land. Capital is scarce, since it results from past savings, which are small because of the lack of previous economic development. Rates of return to capital are automatically high in the early stages of development, and the marginal returns from the abundant factors are correspondingly low. The abundant factor may be land, as in the case of Canada a hundred years ago, or labor, as

[1] This historical model of international capital flows has been widely discussed among economists for some time, but its origin is far from clear. It can be found in an abbreviated form in Paul Samuelson, *Economics*, 10th ed. (New York: McGraw-Hill, 1976), pp. 660-61.

in the case of India more recently. If political or other factors do not intervene, such a country will naturally attract capital inflows during the early stages of its development. These inflows make it possible for a capital-scarce country to invest considerably more than it saves and hence to increase the size of its productive capital stock more rapidly than would otherwise be possible.

As the capital stock grows, however, changes occur in the economy that will eventually reduce or eliminate the inflow of funds. The increase in the capital/labor ratio resulting from the inflow of funds and from the relatively rapid growth of the capital stock raises the marginal return from labor and hence the equilibrium wage rate. Increases in returns to labor (and to land as the capital/land ratio rises) raise domestic per capita income and hence the local savings rate. This increase in the percentage of income saved increases the amount of investment that can be financed domestically and reduces the need for external funds. In addition, the increase in the capital/labor ratio (and in the capital/land ratio) reduces the marginal return from capital and hence the interest or profit rate. This process of "capital deepening," made possible by large capital inflows, ultimately reduces returns to capital and hence the attraction for additional funds. At some point the combination of increased domestic savings and reduced returns to new investments ends the attraction for net capital inflows; the process is then reversed. Savings rates become sufficient both to finance the new investments that are attractive at market interest rates and to repay or repatriate previous capital inflows. In this historical approach, capital flows are determined primarily by an economy's stage of development, with capital inflows occurring early in the process, to be replaced later by capital outflows as the success of the development process makes it possible to repay previous borrowings and, later still, perhaps, by the establishment of a net creditor position relative to the rest of the world.

In this model there is a progression from borrowing to repayment and then to net lending to the rest of the world; this progression ought to parallel a country's development. There are several reasons, however, why a country's progression from the first stage onward may be restrained, so that net borrowing continues despite what appears to be a highly successful development experience.

First, the country's resource base and pattern of comparative advantage may make its development unusually capital-intensive. Returns to additional investment may remain high enough to attract external investment despite a long period of heavy investment financed both with external funds and through increases in domestic savings. An endowment of mineral and land resources spread over vast distances in an inhospitable climate might produce this situation. Most resource industries are inherently capital- rather than labor-intensive, and their capital intensity would obviously be increased by remoteness from markets, necessitating an expensive transportation system, and by a harsh climate, which significantly increases construction costs.

Second, the previous discussion implicitly assumed that the labor force was constant, or at least that it grew only slowly through natural population growth. If, however, heavy immigration occurs, the labor force grows far more rapidly, and the capital/labor ratio may not fall despite a high rate of investment. If a rapidly growing labor force produces a capital/labor ratio that does not fall, there is no reason for returns to capital to fall; the attraction to external funds therefore continues. This is particularly true if workers arriving from abroad typically bring little or no capital with them. In this situation a country may import capital for long periods despite rapid economic growth. Capital inflows create job opportunities, and these in turn attract more immigrants. The only fixed factors of production are land or natural resources; and as long as they remain abundant, the economy can grow quite rapidly without labor shortages or declining profit rates.

Finally, government policies or other factors may reduce the rate of domestic savings so that external financing is needed even late in the development process. If, for example, the public sector dissaves by running chronic budget deficits, the availability of domestic funds for the financing of productive investment is reduced, and reliance on external funding is increased. The domestic savings available for private investment consist of all private savings *minus* public sector deficits. Heavy and chronic deficits produce a "crowding-out" process in domestic capital markets, which means that capital inflows will continue long after they otherwise would have ended.

To summarize, net capital flows result from any of a number of forces producing significant differences in returns to capital in various countries or producing investment levels in excess of domestic savings in some countries, even if free capital mobility produces a common interest rate via arbitrage. Differences in the ratio of the capital stock to supplies of other factors of production are probably the dominant cause of such differences in yields. These differences in relative factor supplies may be the result of different stages in the development process, with capital inflows associated with a developing economy and outflows with a more mature society. In addition to the relative maturities of the relevant economies, other factors may affect the incentives for capital flows. A particularly capital-intensive natural resource base may require external funding despite a sustained rapid rate of economic growth. In addition, a continuing rapid rate of immigration may maintain the capital/labor ratio, and hence relative rates of return to capital, despite heavy capital inflows and fairly high domestic savings. Finally, chronic public sector dissaving may crowd out financing of private investments despite relatively high rates of private savings and may make external funding necessary for normal growth in a relatively mature economy.

Domestic Effects of International Financial Integration

International movements of capital are widely viewed by economists as benefiting both the recipient and the investing country. If interest rates or profit rates accurately reflect the marginal product or real rate of return to capital, a situation in which these rates of return differ significantly between two countries offers sizable opportunities for gains in efficiency, and hence in output, through movements of capital from the low- to the high-return economy. If, for example, returns to capital are 10 percent in one country and 15 percent in another, the opportunity exists for net gains of 5 percent on money moving between the two countries. If the flows are large enough to eliminate the yield differential via arbitrage, so that a joint return of, say, 12 percent prevails in both countries, the net gains are divided between two countries, as suggested in Figure 1.[2]

If the amount of capital *BA* moves from the United States to Canada, reducing U.S. capital stock from *OA* to *OB* and increasing Canadian capital stock from *OC* to *OD,* the U.S. rate of return on capital rises from 10 percent to 12 percent, while the Canadian yield falls from 15 percent to 12 percent. Canadian output increases by the area *CDJI,* which is the amount of capital flowing in times the marginal product of that capital. The return to U.S. investors on this capital is 12 percent times the amount of capital moved, or the area *BAFG.* This area is equal to area *CDJH,* which is what Canada pays out as interest. The net gain for Canada is the remaining shaded triangle *HJI,* which is simply the total return on the capital minus the interest paid to U.S. investors. The U.S. economy lost output equal to area *BAEG* when capital left for Canada, but received a return on its Canadian investment equal to area *BAFG,* for a net gain equivalent to the shaded triangle *EFG.* This triangle is the difference between what the capital yielded in the United States (area *BAEG*) and what it yields in Canada (area *BAFG*). When capital moves in response to the type of yield differential described in the graph, both economies gain. As a result of this type of argument, there is a strong presumption among economists that capital mobility is a good thing and that controls on capital flows are as inefficient as restrictions on trade.

Although this argument is sound, it omits a great deal. It is merely a partial analysis in that it ignores a range of potential side effects or spillovers in both economies that can greatly complicate

---

[2] G. C. Hufbauer, "The Multinational Corporation and Direct Investment," in Peter Kenen, ed., *International Trade and Finance: Frontiers for Research* (Cambridge, Mass.: Cambridge University Press, 1975), p. 291.

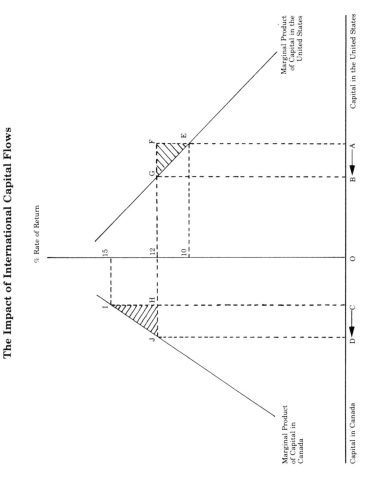

FIGURE 1

The Impact of International Capital Flows

the arguments for mutual welfare gains. A case can still be made for free capital movements, but it is somewhat more complex and rests on some unprovable judgments about the relative importance of these side effects.

The first complication is taxes. The analysis presented in the graph implicitly assumes that U.S. investors, and hence the U.S. economy, received the full 12 percent return on their capital. If part of that return goes to various levels of the Canadian government in the form of taxes, however, it becomes less certain that the U.S. economy really gains from allowing private investment in Canada. For purposes of the example, let us assume that a capital flow in the form of U.S. direct investment in Canada occurs and that both countries have a corporate tax rate of 50 percent. If the capital invested in the United States were yielding 10 percent, half of which went to the government, the private rate of return would be 5 percent. If the direct investment in Canada has a yield of 15 percent, half of which becomes Canadian-government revenue, the private rate of return to the U.S. investor is 7-$\frac{1}{2}$ percent. Comparing after-tax returns, the private investor gains 2-$\frac{1}{2}$ percent by moving funds to Canada. World or total efficiency gains arise because capital shifts from a use in which it returns 10 percent to one in which it yields 15 percent. However, the only problem is that, despite the gains in world efficiency and to the U.S. investor, the U.S. economy loses from this transaction. When the capital is invested in the United States, it yields 10 percent to the economy, with this return's being split between the private investor and the government. When the funds move to Canada, the total yield to the U.S. economy falls to 7-$\frac{1}{2}$ percent. The investor gains 2-$\frac{1}{2}$ percent, but the U.S. government loses 5 percent, which was its previous tax yield on the domestic investment. Ottawa picks up a 7-$\frac{1}{2}$ percent return in the form of taxes, but this is of no value to Washington.[3]

Investment flows of capital from one country to another involve parties other than the investor and typically cost the government of the investing country losses in tax revenues. If all the profits earned from U.S.-owned capital, wherever located, were taxable by the U.S. government at its current rate of 48 percent, Washington would obviously take in much greater revenues than it does, but the result would be double taxation and a virtual end to outflows of direct-investment capital from the United States.

If double taxation were avoided, both world welfare and private profits would improve as a result of free capital mobility, but it is not clear that the investing economy as a whole would also improve, and it is quite likely that the government of the investing country would lose. The exact results depend on tax rates in the two countries and on existing tax treaties. The problem is much less severe for

---

[3] For a more complete discussion of this issue, see Hufbauer, *op. cit.*, pp. 294-301.

debt than for equity capital, since taxes on interest payments to foreign investors are typically much lower than on corporate income. If the Canadian government receives, in the form of withholding taxes, only 10 or 15 percent of the interest payments to Americans, the likelihood of a measurable net loss to the U.S. economy from U.S. investments in Canadian bonds is greatly reduced. Because corporate tax rates are much higher, however, the problem is greater for direct-investment income; this has been one factor leading to proposals in the United States for restrictions on outflows of direct investment in order to keep the funds, and hence the tax base, within the country.

Internal Income-Distribution Effects

The effect of large flows of capital on the distribution of income between capital and labor is another factor complicating the earlier conclusion that capital flows produce welfare benefits for both economies. When small flows of capital are considered, the interest rates and wage rates in each country can be assumed to be unaffected — income-distribution effects are therefore small or nonexistent. However, when capital flows from one country to another are sufficient to significantly affect the capital/labor ratio in either country or in both countries, these flows will also have an impact on interest or profit rates and on wage rates. This means that the distribution of income between capital and labor is affected, which raises welfare, and hence political, problems.[4]

One of the more basic conclusions of price theory is that the marginal product of labor, and hence the equilibrium wage rate, is directly related to the capital/labor ratio. In simpler terms, the more capital used per worker, the higher the worker's productivity and the higher the wage rate. If the flow of capital from the United States to Canada (or to other countries) is sufficient to significantly reduce the U.S. capital/labor ratio, it will reduce the equilibrium wage rate in the United States. If the capital/labor ratio in Canada is significantly increased by capital inflows, the equilibrium wage rate will rise. Returns to capital are also affected in both countries, with the reduced capital/labor ratio in the United States leading to increased equilibrium interest rates and equilibrium profit rates, while these rates decline in Canada because of an increase in the capital/labor ratio there. A major flow of capital from the United States to Canada rewards the owners of that U.S. capital, but imposes losses on U.S. labor. In Canada, the labor force gains while pre-existing owners of Canadian capital lose.

This argument has implicitly assumed that wage rates are fully flexible and adjust quickly to clear the labor market in each country.

---

[4] R. Albert Berry and Ronald Soligo, "Some Welfare Aspects of International Migration," *Journal of Political Economy*, September-October, 1969, pp. 778-95.

If the more realistic Keynesian assumption of rigid short-run wage rates and significant unemployment is adopted, the large capital flows affect the level of employment in each country rather than the wage rate. An increase in the Canadian capital/labor ratio raises the productivity of, and the demand for, local labor. The result is a decline in the unemployment rate. In the United States the opposite occurs. The decline in the capital/labor ratio reduces the productivity of, and the demand for, labor. Since wage rates do not fall, the result is a higher unemployment rate. Whether the adjustment process occurs through changes in wage rates or in unemployment levels (or, more realistically, in both), the conclusion is the same: workers in Canada gain and workers in the United States lose when large amounts of capital flow north.

These income-distribution effects complicate the classical argument for free capital mobility. Although efficiency and total output in the combined economy of the two countries are increased, some groups lose — workers in the United States and pre-existing owners of capital in Canada, for example. The question then becomes how to weight these income losses against the gains received by workers in Canada and by U.S. owners of capital. If one could assume that a dollar in income has the same value or utility to any recipient, the classical conclusion could be maintained because total output, and total incomes, would go up. Unfortunately, there is no way to defend that particular assumption and no way to know how the value of an extra dollar in income for one person compares with the value received from the same dollar by another. The impossibility of objective interpersonal comparisons of this sort produces a very uncertain conclusion. Although free capital mobility increases total output and total incomes, there is no way of knowing whether it actually increases the total welfare of the two countries. One may have opinions on how the losses of U.S. workers compare with the gains to Canadian workers, but an objective measurement of welfare effects on the two groups is not possible.

One thing, however, is clear. U.S. labor unions will oppose net outflows of capital from the United States with some vigor for the same reasons that they oppose free trade. Since labor is the relatively scarce, and expensive, factor of production in the United States, either free trade or free capital mobility will tend to reduce U.S. wage rates. The AFL-CIO may seem narrow and even isolationist in its protectionism and in its opposition to U.S. direct investment abroad, but the federation is accurately reflecting its (U.S.) members' interests in both instances. The leaders of U.S. unions are not elected to represent the interests of world efficiency.

In addition to the purely economic effects of large capital flows, some social and political effects of such flows should also be noted briefly. Although the recipient country (and workers and government tax receipts in particular) may gain in economic terms from major capital inflows, non-economic side effects may occur that appear, at least to some people, to offset income increases. Most people are nationalistic to some degree and are uncomfortable with the presence of large or dominant foreign businesses in their country. A great deal has been written about the rise of Canadian nationalism and particularly about the strong opposition to the presence of large U.S. firms in Canada. This phenomenon is not restricted to Canada. The recent increase in the number of foreign firms investing in the United States, for example, has caused a considerable stir in some political circles there. Whatever the purely economic advantages of capital inflows, they have political or psychological side effects that are not always, or even typically, positive. For whatever reasons, many people are uneasy about an influx of major foreign investors, giving rise to the question of how these intangible effects are to be weighted in comparison with the economic benefits of capital inflows. The only possible answer is that such a weighting process is inherently political and therefore outside the competence of economics, or at least of economic theory.

Two-Directional Capital Flows or International Financial Intermediation

Although it makes intuitive sense that funds flow from capital-abundant to capital-scarce countries in response to yield differentials, it is not obvious why capital ought to flow in both directions between national financial markets. Capital often, or even typically, flows in both directions across the Canadian-U.S. border, flowing south in one form and north in another.

Sometimes capital flows in both directions in very similar forms, such as when U.S. banks are extending loans to Canadian corporate customers at the same time that Canadian banks are making similar loans to customers in the United States, or when Canadian and U.S. investors are purchasing equities or other securities in each other's markets. The same relationship, although usually on a lesser scale, exists among other sets of countries. This type of relationship suggests a far more complete integration of the capital markets of the two countries than is indicated by the one-directional capital flows discussed earlier. The causes of such extensive integration of different national capital markets are also far more complex than those of one-directional capital flows.

There is no single cause, such as yield differentials reflecting relative national scarcities of capital, to explain extensive two-way capital flows, since such relative scarcities could hardly cause flows of funds in both directions between the same two countries. There are, instead, numerous factors or circumstances that have to be taken into account. The following discussion, although not exhaustive, will attempt to highlight what appear to be the dominant factors encouraging such developments. Although this section is not intended to relate narrowly and specifically to the Canadian-U.S. experience, the choice of topics for treatment is hardly accidental. It is designed to provide background for the later discussion of the specifics of the relationship between the capital markets of these two countries and will consequently stress those elements particularly relevant to that relationship. These factors also exist in other bilateral financial relationships, but the weighting or relative importance differs in other cases.

The existence of capital flows in both directions between two national capital markets implies that, for some reason, one market is acting as a financial intermediary between lenders and borrowers in the other country. If, for example, short-term funds flow from Canada to the United States while long-term capital flows in the opposite direction, U.S. financial markets are acting as intermediaries between Canadian lenders who want to hold relatively liquid short-term assets and Canadian borrowers who want funds for longer periods of time. This conclusion could be reversed, however, by suggesting that Canadian financial markets are acting as intermediaries between U.S. lenders who prefer to hold relatively long-term assets and U.S. borrowers who want funds for shorter periods. Whichever way it is viewed, a situation in which short-term funds flow south and long-term funds flow north represents the provision of intermediating services by one economy to lenders and borrowers in the other. Since financial intermediaries are typically viewed as institutions that borrow short and lend long, thereby bridging the gap between the desire of savers for liquidity and the need of borrowers for longer maturities, the situation in which short-term funds flow from Toronto to New York and return as loans with longer maturities is most reasonably viewed in terms of U.S. capital markets' acting as intermediaries between Canadian lenders and borrowers, rather than the reverse.

The question, then, is why such patterns of flows exist — that is, why the capital markets of one country provide such intermediating services for another. At its most basic level, this process requires a combination of low transactions and information costs, together with some significant difference in the structures or performances of the two capital markets. If government legislation or other impediments make it difficult or expensive to move funds or if information about yields and risks does not cross borders easily, such integration is impossible, or at least highly unlikely, despite other differences between the two markets. If, however, the two capital markets were exactly alike in terms of the structures of yields, costs of doing business, risks, and the behavior of asset prices, there would be no incentive for capital to flow in either direction. Transactions and information costs are never zero for international dealings, so if some differences in yield structures or in other conditions facing market participants in the two countries do not exist, capital flows will obviously not occur.

The forces encouraging capital-market integration are analogous to those encouraging international trade in the standard theory of comparative advantage: a combination of low transportation and information costs and differences in the ratios of prices for some pairs of goods in different countries. The only difference is that, in the case of capital markets, the trade involves different types of financial assets rather than wine and cloth — the typical pair of goods in textbook examples of comparative advantage.

Yield Curves

There are a number of differences between two sets of capital markets that can create incentives for two-directional capital flows. The most important and most obvious are variations in the structure of yields. Such differences may exist even if the two countries have the same average yields on capital, in that yields on one type of asset may typically be higher in one country, while yields on another type of asset may be higher in the other. There might, for example, be a tendency for yields on equities to be relatively high in the United States and yields on long-term bonds to be higher in Canada. Even if average yields in the two markets were the same, Canadian funds would flow south into U.S. common stocks while U.S. funds flowed north into Canadian bonds. As long as transactions and information costs and exchange risks are not zero, these flows will not be sufficient to fully eliminate the yield differentials.

The structure of yields within a set of capital markets can be viewed in terms of a number of dimensions, including type of financial instrument, degree of risk, and length of maturity. One country's capital markets might produce systematically higher risk premiums than another's, attracting capital inflows into high-risk assets and encouraging outflows into low-risk foreign investments. The most important dimension of yield structures, however, is probably maturity, or what is commonly referred to as the slope of the yield curve.

For a variety of reasons, including relative liquidity and risk of price changes, long-term bonds typically carry significantly higher yields than do short-term liabilities issued by the same borrower. If interest rates facing a given class of borrowers are plotted according to maturity, with very short-term liabilities on the left and long-term bonds on the right, the resulting yield curve will typically have a positive slope, meaning that the interest cost of borrowing increases with the maturity of the debt. The steepness of the yield curve, however, varies over time and often varies among countries. If, for example, the yield curve is typically steeper in Canada than in the United States (which has historically been the case) — meaning that the extra cost of long-term borrowing was greater in Canada than in the United States — then, even if the two countries had the same *average* yields, short-term funds would flow from Canada to the United States, while long-term funds would flow in the opposite direction. Each flow would be in response to yield differentials for that particular class of asset, with the steeper Canadian yield curve encouraging an outflow of short-term funds and a simultaneous inflow of longer-term funds. As noted earlier, such differences in the structure of yields could exist with regard to risk of default or to type of financial instrument, as well as with regard to maturity. Any of these differences would produce two-directional capital flows and the resulting provision of intermediary services by one set of capital markets for lenders and borrowers in the other.

To conclude that two-directional capital flows are caused by differing yield structures does not really explain why these flows occur, because it ignores the reasons for differing yield structures in the first place. The ultimate cause of the international intermediation process lies in the various forces that produce a consistent pattern of yields on various assets in one country that differs significantly from the pattern in another country. The issue of most direct interest here is why the yield curve might be consistently steeper in one country than in another — that is, why the margin between long- and short-term yields in two countries might differ in a fairly consistent way.

The steepness of a yield curve is widely viewed as reflecting expected rates of inflation. A steep yield curve implies that investors expect an increase in the rate of inflation, and hence an increase in the nominal interest rates required to maintain real yields. The expected increase in interest rates leads them to remain as liquid as possible in order to avoid capital losses on bonds, the prices of which will decline with higher interest rates. If people expect the inflation rate to climb, they will expect interest rates to rise and bond prices to fall. In such a situation they avoid holding bonds and instead concentrate on short-term assets in their portfolios. If large numbers of investors hold such expectations, there will be selling pressure in bond markets, driving prices down, and a strong demand for short-term assets, driving prices up. The decline in bond prices means higher yields, and vice versa for short-term assets, so the yield curve becomes steeper. If Canada's yield curve is steeper than that prevailing in the United States, it might merely suggest that at that time Canadian investors expected an increase in the rate of inflation, while investors in the United States did not.[5]

---

[5] For a review of this and related theories of the determination of the term structure of interest rates in the Canadian context, see K. A. Stroatman, "The Theory of Long-Term International Capital Flows and Canadian Corporate Debt Issues in the United States" (Ph.D. dissertation, University of British Columbia, May, 1974), pp.

Such differences in inflation expectations can explain temporary shifts in the yield curve in Canada relative to the United States, but they can be responsible for long-standing differences in the steepness of yield curves in the two countries only if investors in one have a permanent expectation that the rate of inflation will increase relative to that in the other. This hardly seems likely, since such expectations would have to be disappointed unless inflation consistently escalated in one country or decelerated in the other. This has not happened in either country, so if a difference in the steepness of the yield curves of the two countries persists for a relatively long period, its cause would appear to lie outside the standard "expectations-of-inflation" model.

A steeper yield curve in one country might also reflect an inherently stronger preference for liquidity in that country than in another. Even if supply functions for financial claims in the two countries were identical, a particularly strong preference for safety and liquidity among savers in one country would produce demand functions for assets that were strongly biased toward shorter maturities. If Canadian portfolio managers and individual investors have a stronger liquidity preference than those in the United States, a steeper yield curve will be required in Canada to entice investors to hold a given proportion of long-term assets. The steepness of the yield curve is the compensation provided to an investor for giving up the liquidity and safety of short-term assets.

A particularly strong national preference for liquidity could have a number of sources, including banking traditions that strongly discourage long-term loans in favor of shorter-term commitments. Its source might also lie in the regulatory process. If regulatory agencies impose secondary reserve requirements or other liquidity requirements on banks and on other financial institutions, the result must be a reduction in the demand for long-term relative to short-term assets, and thus a steeper yield curve. Finally, historical or cultural forces in one country may make its investors more comfortable with relatively liquid portfolios than are investors in another country. This means that a steeper yield curve will be necessary in the former country to entice investors to hold a given proportion of their portfolios in the form of long-term, and hence riskier, assets.

These arguments suggest why relative demands for different kinds of assets might differ in two countries. It is also possible, however, that differences exist on the supply side of asset markets. Borrowers in one country might have a stronger preference for long-term funds, perhaps because of the nature of their businesses, while borrowers in another country might be more willing to borrow in the short-term market. If such a difference existed, the greater relative supply of

---

14-70. A review of the theory and econometric estimates can also be found in F. Modigliani and R. J. Shiller, "Inflation, Rational Expectations and the Term Structure of Interest Rates," *Economica*, February, 1973, pp. 12-43.

long-term assets in the former country would depress bond prices, thereby raising their yields and producing a steeper yield curve.

The most obvious reason for such differences in borrowers' maturity preferences would be differences in the types of expenditures being financed with the borrowed funds. This might, in turn, represent basic differences in the structures or stages of development of the two economies. If, for example, the rapidly growing sector of one economy were that comprising manufacturing or resource industries, which require massive plant and equipment expenditures with relatively long payback periods, borrowers in that economy would be looking primarily for long-term funds. If the leading growth sector of the other economy were services or retail trade, where plant and equipment expenditures are less important but working capital is vital, the result would be a heavy demand for short-term funds. In this case, the first country would have a steeper yield curve than the second, even if the demand sides of the asset markets were identical.

Legal or institutional factors can also affect relative supplies for long-term and short-term assets. If, for example, a transactions tax existed on new issues or if the other costs of bringing an issue to market were higher in one country, borrowers would be strongly encouraged to operate at the long end of the market to avoid paying the tax or extra costs more than once when maturing short-term issues were refinanced or rolled over. High transactions costs in capital markets will generally encourage long-term borrowing and a somewhat steeper yield curve.

The previous two arguments have suggested how differences in the structure of asset demands in the two economies and differences in the supply functions for financial assets might cause differences in the steepness of the yield curves in the two countries. A relatively steep yield curve is caused either by institutional and individual investors having a particularly strong preference for highly liquid portfolios or by borrowers having an equally strong preference for long-term financing. There is another factor causing a relatively steep yield curve that combines the two sides of the market by simultaneously affecting supply and demand functions for financial assets. If a capital market is relatively small or thin, and particularly if secondary markets are relatively illiquid and unpredictable, both borrowers and lenders will be encouraged to behave in a way that produces a steep yield curve. From the perspective of the lender, a thin or immature capital market means that it may be very difficult or costly to sell assets before maturity. Thin secondary markets strongly encourage lenders to accept maturities that are no longer than the period for which it is certain that the funds will not be needed. In a broad, mature capital market, however, lenders are more confident of their ability to sell marketable securities quickly and at little risk. This means that lenders are encouraged by a thin, illiquid secondary market to hold far more liquid portfolios than are investors in a broad, liquid capital market. Asset demand is shifted toward shorter maturities in the former case and toward longer maturities in the latter. The result is a steeper yield curve in the smaller and less liquid capital market.

The same forces operate for borrowers. In a broad and liquid market, credit-worthy borrowers are relatively certain of their ability to roll over or refinance maturing debt and so are willing to borrow at maturities that are shorter than the period for which the funds will be needed if short-term interest rates are attractive. For a rational borrower the choice of maturities can be based largely on relative interest rates and on expectations for future yields, rather than on the period for which the funds are needed. The certainty that new financing will be available when debt matures makes this possible. In a thin, illiquid market, however, borrowers are necessarily much less certain that they will be able to refinance maturing debt and are strongly encouraged to borrow for the full period during which funds will be needed. Rolling over one-year notes to finance a factory that will be amortized over ten years is feasible in the first case, but very risky in the second. As a result, borrowers are pushed toward the longer maturities in the thin, illiquid capital market, but are much more likely to accept shorter maturities in the mature and broad market.

When the effects of illiquid capital markets on borrowers and on lenders are combined, the result is a strong argument for a steep yield curve. In a relatively immature or illiquid capital market, lenders are encouraged to avoid long-term assets by uncertainty over prospects for selling them in thin secondary markets prior to maturity. Similarly, borrowers are encouraged by their uncertain prospects for refinancing maturing debt to find maturities that are fully as long as the period for which funds are needed. Lenders are encouraged to remain at relatively short maturities, while borrowers try to lengthen their maturities, meaning that a steep yield curve is necessary to clear capital markets. One would then expect the steepness of yield curves to vary inversely with the size, breadth, and liquidity of national capital markets.

Put in other terms, if borrowers and lenders are assumed to be risk-averse, unstable yields — and hence asset prices — will encourage both groups to remain as liquid as possible. This means that lenders will avoid large changes in their asset values by holding shorter maturities, while borrowers will avoid great uncertainty in interest costs by arranging the longest possible maturities. Again, highly uncertain or unstable capital markets encourage steep yield curves. Whether the maturity of a capital market is defined in terms of the nature of secondary markets and the certainty with which maturing debt can be promptly refinanced or in terms of the stability of yields and asset prices, the result is the same. Immature, thin, and relatively illiquid capital markets produce steep yield curves. When capital can move between such a market and one that is significantly broader and more liquid, and where the yield curve is therefore flatter, there is a natural pattern of capital flows. Short-term funds will flow from the illiquid market to the more liquid one, and long-term funds will flow in the opposite direction. The result will be that the illiquidity of the former market will be partially eased by having the other act as an intermediary.

By borrowing short and lending long, and hence acting as an intermediary, the more liquid capital market is partially bridging the gap between the desires of borrowers and those of lenders in the less liquid market. In that sense it is providing the liquidity that the other market lacks and hence "imports." The cost of this import is the difference between the long-term yields at which the more liquid market lends and the short-term interest rates at which it borrows. That differential is the net yield to the more liquid market from this process — that is, the price of the liquidity imported by the smaller and less mature capital market. The process of international financial integration can then be viewed in part as the sale of intermediation services, and hence of liquidity, by mature, broad, and relatively liquid capital markets to less mature, thinner, and less liquid markets. In domestic finance the role of a financial intermediary is to provide additional liquidity to borrowers and to lenders by selling relatively liquid liabilities and by purchasing less liquid assets. To the extent that this intermediation process is incomplete or less than fully successful within a national capital market, the resulting lack of liquidity can be eliminated or eased through international financial integration.

The relative efficiency or competitiveness of a capital market may have the same effect on the yield curve as breadth and liquidity — that is, the less competitive or efficient the market, the steeper the yield curve is likely to be. Financial intermediaries in general, and banks in particular, borrow short-term funds and lend at somewhat longer maturities. The margin between the short-term interest rates at which they borrow and the longer-term yields at which they lend is the source of their revenues, from which costs must be covered and any profit earned. In a capital market consisting largely of such institutions, the relationship between long-term and short-term yields will depend, in part, on the costs of running these intermediaries and on the profit rates they typically earn. If intermediaries are inefficient or uncompetitive, they will offer relatively low returns to lenders of short-term funds and demand higher interest rates from longer-term borrowers, producing a relatively steep yield curve. The more efficient and competitive a capital market becomes, the more intermediaries will bid for short-term funds and the less they will charge for longer-term funds. The reduced margin between what the intermediaries pay for short-term funds and what they get for long-term loans denotes a flatter yield curve.

In the case of the inefficient or uncompetitive capital market with the steeper yield curve, the role of international financial integration is to provide outside competition for local intermediaries. The steep local yield curve will encourage foreign financial institutions to borrow short from, and lend long to, that market, thus acting as a competitive intermediary. The ability of domestic intermediaries to remain less efficient or more profitable than those in other national capital markets is greatly limited by this process of financial integration. The greater the degree of integration and the lower the transactions costs of international capital flows, the more local intermediaries will be forced to match or approximate the efficiency and competitive behavior of financial institutions in other capital markets. Intermediation services can be imported like shoes. If the local intermediaries are high-cost operations, they will encounter the same sort of competition faced by high-cost shoe companies. Actually, the competition will be worse, because most industrialized countries have tariffs on shoes, but not on flows of capital.

One major result of capital-market integration should be to reduce the difference between Canadian and U.S. yield curves. The flow of short-term funds to the south should increase money-market yields in Toronto and reduce them in New York. The flow of long-term funds in the opposite direction should increase bond yields in New York and reduce them in Toronto. The relative size of the two capital markets would suggest that most of the interest-rate changes will occur in Canada — that is, the Canadian yield curve will become flatter as a result of these capital flows. If transactions costs, exchange-rate risks, and costs of information were zero, a process of arbitrage should produce a Canadian yield curve exactly duplicating that prevailing in New York. These costs and risks are obviously not zero, so such "perfect" integration of capital markets is only a theoretical abstraction. It remains true, however, that any increase in the level of capital-market integration should reduce the extent to which the yield curves of two countries are apt to differ.

The discussion thus far would appear to imply that two-directional capital flows are encouraged by differences in the structures of asset yields among countries, with maturity being the dominant variable in these structures. While it is probably true that differences in the steepness of yield curves comprise the *single* most important factor encouraging two-directional capital flows, there are circumstances other than yield structures capable of producing such results and therefore deserving attention.

Market Size As a Cause of Capital Flows

Capital will sometimes flow from a large capital market to a small one despite the lack of obvious yield incentives — for example, when the existence of very large domestic borrowers and relatively small capital markets makes it impossible to find sufficient funds in domestic financial institutions. For reasons of safety, financial intermediaries typically put a fairly strict limit on the percentage of their assets that represents claims on a single borrower. When a country's capital markets and financial institutions are relatively small compared to that country's large borrowers, totally domestic financing may become impossible, irrespective of yields and credit-worthiness. The maximum acceptable size of a single domestic bond issue, for example, is a function of the size of the local capital market; and if major borrowers typically need more than that maximum, they will be compelled to borrow in New York or London, irrespective of yield. The large capital market again provides intermediation services for the smaller market, but in this case the determining factor is the ability to accommodate particularly large borrowers rather than the margin between short-term and long-term yields.

Regulation and Capital Flows

Regulatory policies may also encourage capital flows that are not based on differentials in market-determined yields. Insurance companies, for example, are usually required to maintain assets in each country in which they do business that are proportional to their policy liabilities in that country. Since Canadian and U.S. insurance companies do business in both countries, they must maintain large portfolios in both. As a result, Canadian insurance companies may be making sizable investments in the U.S. bond market at the same time that U.S. insurance companies are taking equally large positions in Canadian securities. Each investment is based on regulatory policies and on the companies' policy liabilities in the other country rather than on relative yields.

Regulation Q in the United States provides another example of regulation-induced capital flows. Under that rule the interest rates that U.S. banks can pay on domestic short-term deposits have been strictly limited. When market yields on such deposits exceed the legal maximum, foreign banks, including those from Canada, are able to attract deposits from the United States and relend the funds in the New York market quite profitably. The New York agencies of Canadian banks, for example, have often attracted U.S.-dollar deposits, which they then place on deposit in Toronto or Montreal, thus escaping the U.S. regulations. The funds are subsequently loaned back to the agency in New York, which lends them to brokers and other short-term borrowers.

In this instance Canadian banks are intermediating in the United States by borrowing short-term funds from, and lending them back to, this market. This is caused not by market forces, but rather by U.S. regulations that interfere with the market determination of yields on bank deposits in the United States. The growth of the Euro-dollar market was probably encouraged more by Regulation Q than by any other single factor.[6] By prohibiting U.S. banks from paying competitive interest rates on short-term deposits in periods of tight monetary policy, Regulation Q discouraged both U.S. citizens and foreigners from maintaining such deposits in the United States. The result was a profitable opportunity to create an offshore, and hence unregulated, U.S.-dollar banking industry. U.S.-dollar banking in Canada was part of the response to that opportunity, and the London Euro-dollar market was a later but much larger response.

Direct Investments

Direct investments in wholly- or majority-owned subsidiaries by domestic corporations represent another situation where capital flows in both directions across the border, often against what would appear to be the incentives of relative average profit rates. U.S. firms may be making investments in Canadian facilities or lending funds to Canadian subsidiaries despite average profit rates in Canada lower than those in the United States. At the same time, Canadian firms may be involved in similar activities in the United States in the opposite direction.

The explanation of this instance of two-directional capital flows is that direct investments represent a package of capital, technology, marketing abilities, and management. The *average* profit rate in Canada may be lower than that prevailing in the United States, but the rate of return in Canada for a particular U.S. firm whose technology, product, and marketing skills are unique, or at least unusual, may be much higher than the Canadian or U.S. average. Simultaneously, a Canadian firm in a different industry may have opportunities in the United States that are far more profitable than those facing other U.S. firms, for the same reasons. Direct-investment flows are not responses to differentials in average profit rates in the two countries; rather, they result from particular opportunities facing individual firms that often have unique technical or managerial assets. For tax and other reasons, direct-investment flows are often augmented by debt capital as parent firms lend to their existing foreign subsidiaries rather than make increased equity investments. The result is that long-term debt capital often flows in both directions across a border as parent firms in each country lend to their subsidiaries in the other.

Risk Reduction Through International Portfolio Diversification

The final cause of international financial intermediation is the spreading of risks through the distribution of a portfolio among assets originating in a number of countries. Institutional and individual investors presumably operate with two goals — the

---

[6] Milton Friedman, "The Euro-Dollar Market: Some First Principles," *Morgan Guaranty Survey*, October, 1969, pp. 4-14.

maximization of returns and the avoidance of large risks of capital loss. These two goals often conflict because long-term and otherwise risky assets typically offer significantly higher yields than do short-term assets with low risks of default. The result is that those managing portfolios must reach compromises or trade-offs in pursuing these two goals. One of the obvious and most important ways of reducing risks without great sacrifice of yield is to spread a portfolio among many different kinds of assets, thereby avoiding an excessive holding of the liabilities of any one borrower.

One of the problems in reducing risks through such portfolio management is that most long-term assets in a single country tend to follow roughly parallel price patterns. All long-term bonds decline in price, imposing losses on their holders, when interest rates rise, so risks resulting from cyclical movements in interest rates are not significantly reduced by spreading a portfolio among bonds issued by a number of firms or governments in one country. Risks of default are reduced by such an investment pattern, but risks of loss due to interest-rate changes and their effects on bond prices are not. Since prices of common and preferred stocks tend to follow bond prices with a short lag, losses on equities usually accompany losses on bond holdings. If the stock market declines shortly after bond prices decline, portfolio risks have not been greatly reduced by holding equities as well as long-term debt. There are some assets, such as real estate, gold, and short-term money-market instruments (or cash) whose values do not parallel those of long-term bonds, but portfolio managers operating only within one economy do have a problem in trying to spread their holdings across a range of assets to reduce risks. Too many asset prices follow parallel patterns over cycles in monetary policy, declining in periods of tight money and rising when monetary policy becomes less restrictive.

Distributing a portfolio among assets in countries typically having at least somewhat different business and monetary-policy cycles is a potentially important way of dealing with this problem. Holding a range of U.S. long-term assets does not reduce risks of cyclical changes in asset prices, but holding only part of the portfolio in U.S. assets and spreading the rest across Canada, Germany, Japan, the United Kingdom, and so forth, does reduce these risks.[7] As long as these countries do not have exactly parallel patterns of monetary policy, and hence of long-term asset prices, investors can reduce risks considerably by spreading their holdings across a number of currencies and countries. When U.S. monetary policy is tight, resulting in losses on the U.S. portion of the portfolio, German interest rates may be falling, resulting in higher asset prices and profits on

---

[7] Herbert Grubel, "Internationally Diversified Portfolios," *American Economic Review*, December, 1968, pp. 1299-1314. For a less technical discussion of the same topic, see Herbert Grubel, *International Economics* (Homewood, Illinois: Richard D. Irwin and Co., 1977), pp. 536-43.

that part of the portfolio. When the U.K. part of the portfolio is doing badly, Japanese assets may be doing better, and vice versa. Exchange risks are also reduced this way, because when one currency is rising, others are likely to be falling. For example, the reputed stability of Special Drawing Rights (SDRs) is readily available to portfolio managers simply by spreading their assets among investments denominated in the sixteen currencies used in determining the value of SDRs in accordance with their relative weights.

Risks resulting from interest-rate changes and their effects on long-term asset prices are reduced only to the extent that the patterns of monetary policy in the various countries differ. If all industrialized countries followed the same monetary policy, there would be a parallel movement of interest rates and asset prices in these economies, and a portfolio manager would not reduce his risks significantly by spreading assets among a number of countries. A portfolio manager's ideal would be to discover two countries that always followed opposite monetary policies. If one country were always easing monetary policy when the other was tightening, and vice versa, asset prices would always rise in one country when they were falling in the other, and vice versa. The investor could simply split his portfolio between these two countries and largely forget about the effects of business and monetary-policy cycles on the value of his holdings. There is no such pair of countries, however, because events in one country will often produce a roughly parallel business cycle in all, or at least the vast majority of, the other industrialized countries. OPEC price increases and the resulting 1975 recession in all the major industrialized countries represented an unhappy but obvious example of such parallelism. It is more common, however, for at least some differences in the cyclical and monetary-policy experiences of the major countries to exist. It is obviously impossible to find countries that always, or even typically, follow opposite patterns, but it is possible to find economies whose cyclical experiences usually differ to some degree. As a result, it is possible to reduce cyclical risks in a portfolio by spreading them among assets denominated in a variety of currencies from a number of different countries.

Portfolio managers will typically shift the proportion of their assets in different countries with changes in relative interest rates and with changes in expectations for future exchange-rate and interest-rate changes. They will not, however, put all their assets in one or two countries, or totally withdraw from a major country, except under very unusual circumstances. As a result, it is not unusual for some money to flow against modest interest-rate differentials, or at least without the incentive of such differentials. As new funds flow into a portfolio, they will be distributed among a number of assets in different countries. Although most of the new money will go where interest rates are highest, the maintenance of a desired portfolio balance will often mean that some of it goes to lower-yield countries.

The result is that international capital flows cannot be viewed solely in terms of investors responding to differences in interest rates. Although capital flows obviously do respond to such differentials, there is a great deal more to it than that. As long as portfolio managers view international diversification as a way of reducing risks, a certain amount of money will flow into countries whose interest rates are not particularly high.

Summary

The determinants of international capital flows and of the pattern of international financial integration are obviously complex. An attempt has been made to identify some of the more important factors, with particular emphasis on those that may be of relevance to the Canadian-U.S. context. Simple interest-rate differentials are of obvious relevance, but differences in the structure of yields in the two economies are probably equally important. In addition, there are a number of factors, such as regulatory policies, the role of the U.S. dollar as an official reserve asset, and the desire of investors to reduce portfolio risks by spreading assets among a number of countries, that often cause capital to flow in patterns that cannot be explained by relative yields alone.

Foreign-Exchange Reserves

The role of the U.S. dollar as the dominant foreign-exchange-reserve asset creates another cause of international capital flows not directly related to yield differentials. If Canada increases its foreign-exchange reserves in the form of liabilities of the U.S. Treasury or of the Federal Reserve System, Canadian capital has flowed to the United States just as certainly as if individual Canadians had deposited money in U.S. commercial banks. The fact that the U.S. dollar has been the major reserve asset since World War II has made it possible for the United States to borrow huge sums from the rest of the world at rather modest interest rates. For a while it was even thought that the reserve role of the U.S. dollar meant that the concept of a balance of payments deficit was meaningless for the United States because any accounting deficit could be financed simply by creating additional U.S.-dollar reserve assets for an eager world to hold.[8] The world became much less eager, and even unwilling, to hold the vast amounts of dollar reserve assets being created by U.S. deficits in the late 1960s, resulting in the devaluation of the dollar on August 15, 1971, and in the adoption of floating exchange rates by many countries in early 1973.

---

[8] Émile Després, Charles Kindleberger, and Walter Salant, "The Dollar and World Liquidity: A Minority View," *The Economist*, February 5, 1966.

Despite these setbacks and widespread expectations that SDRs would soon become the dominant international reserve asset, the U.S. dollar has retained its widespread use as a reserve currency. This means that large amounts of capital flow into the United States whenever other countries have balance of payments surpluses, thereby accumulating additional reserves in the usual form of liabilities of the U.S. Treasury. Such surpluses and the resulting flows of capital into the United States are not the products of interest-rate differentials favoring investments in U.S. assets. The building up of U.S.-dollar reserve assets by countries with fixed exchange rates is a residual or accommodating item in their balances of payments and is caused by the various determinants of all the other items in the balance of payments accounts, including foreign trade and private capital flows.

For countries like Canada, which have a managed floating exchange rate, foreign-exchange-reserve accumulations are not a purely residual or accommodating item in the payments accounts. They are, instead, the result of decisions by government or central banks to intervene in the exchange market in order to determine, or at least to influence, movements of the exchange rate. If the Canadian government decided, for example, to discourage an appreciation of the Canadian dollar, the Bank of Canada would be instructed to purchase U.S. dollars in the exchange market, thereby putting downward pressure on the Canadian dollar. The resulting accumulation of U.S. dollars would represent an addition to Canada's foreign-exchange reserves and would typically be held in the form of U.S. Treasury debt. A capital flow from Canada to the United States would have occurred for reasons that had nothing to do with the attractiveness of U.S. interest rates to Canadian investors. A great deal of capital flows in the form of such reserve accumulations, although the need for these flows was reduced in 1973 with the adoption of managed floating exchange rates by many of the industrialized countries.

Domestic Effects of International Financial Integration

The international integration of capital markets has some important impacts on the independence and effectiveness of domestic monetary policy. In a world of rigidly fixed exchange rates and integrated capital markets, the central bank of a relatively small country has little, if any, real independence in setting monetary policy. Its policies must roughly parallel those in the larger countries with which its domestic capital markets are integrated, because any significant deviation will be made ineffective by a combination of interest arbitrage and the resulting balance of payments effects. If, for example, the Bank of Canada decided to maintain a tight monetary policy while the Federal Reserve System was in an expansionary phase, the result would be significantly higher interest rates in

Canada than in the United States. With fixed exchange rates that were not expected to change, the result would be a large or even massive flow of funds from New York to Toronto, which would significantly reduce the interest-rate differentials. Interest rates in the two markets would approach each other for the same reason that the prices of wheat in two markets converge when arbitrageurs buy in the low-price market and sell in the high-price market. The only difference is that pieces of paper, rather than wheat, are bought and sold, so that the transportation costs are lower. If exchange rates are rigidly fixed and if there is no expectation of change, exchange risk can be ignored, and simple arbitrage can be used to enforce approximate equality in interests rates in the two markets. If there is a small range of exchange-rate variation around a peg, as was the case for the Canadian dollar in 1962-70, when the parity was 92.5¢ and the range of possible market rates was 91.75¢ to 93.25¢, there is some exchange risk, meaning that modest interest-rate differentials can exist without generating overwhelming arbitrage pressures. Even in this case, however, the degree of Canadian interest-rate independence is decidedly limited.

Arbitrage pressure not only enforces a rough equality in interest rates, but also produces balance of payments effects that largely cancel, or at least compromise, the central bank's attempts to control money supply. In the previous case of a tight monetary policy in Canada, the resulting capital inflows will force Canada's balance of payments into a sizable surplus. This will compel official exchange-market intervention whereby the Bank of Canada buys U.S. dollars, which are added to Canada's foreign-exchange reserves, and makes payment in Canadian funds that immediately flow into the commercial banking system. The result is an increase in the Canadian money supply, in clear conflict with the desired restrictive policy. When the Bank of Canada buys U.S. dollars in the exchange market in order to maintain a fixed parity in the face of a payments surplus, it increases the Canadian money supply exactly as if it had bought domestic Treasury bills in a standard expansionary open-market operation. The only differences are that the Bank of Canada bought U.S. dollars rather than domestic Treasury bills and that the policy was not voluntary. The policy was necessitated by the Bank of Canada's need to maintain a fixed exchange rate. The central bank can try to offset the expansionary effects of the payments surplus with a further tightening of domestic monetary policy — a policy known as "sterilization" — but if the capital markets of Canada and the United States are closely integrated, so that a great deal of money will flow in response to sizable interest-rate differentials, the effects of the sterilization policies are likely to be overwhelmed by continuing capital inflows and the resulting payments surplus. In a world of fixed exchange rates and highly integrated capital markets, a small country has little significant monetary independence. When

Canada had a fixed parity in 1962-70, it was known as the "Thirteenth Federal Reserve District" in some circles in the United States. Although the term was unkind, the combination of a fixed parity and the extensive integration of the Canadian and U.S. capital markets meant that it was not unfair.

The adoption of flexible or floating exchange rates changes this situation markedly by making national monetary policy both more independent and more effective. First, a floating exchange rate introduces a greater exchange risk for unhedged capital flows, meaning that the arbitrage mechanism will be far weaker. Market interest rates will not be forced together by uncovered capital flows because the risks of exchange-rate movement make such activities unattractive unless investors are gamblers rather than arbitrageurs. Covered interest-rate differentials will be limited by arbitrage pressures, largely because forward exchange rates will move far enough from prevailing spot rates to offset existing interest-rate margins. If a tight-money policy in Canada produces 9 percent short-term yields, while similar assets yield only 6 percent in the United States, exchange risk will prevent these interest rates from being forced together by uncovered arbitrage. Instead, covered arbitrage flows will produce a 3 percent forward discount on the Canadian dollar, thereby eliminating the covered interest differential. Canada will be able to retain its 9 percent interest rate despite significantly lower yields in New York.

The floating exchange rate also moderates the pressure of a Canadian balance of payments surplus to cause an increase in domestic money supply. Since the Bank of Canada is no longer compelled to defend a parity through exchange-market intervention, it can simply allow the Canadian dollar to appreciate as capital flows respond to the higher Canadian interest rates. There is no compulsory purchase of U.S. dollars with the resulting flow of new Canadian funds into the banking system. The domestic money supply remains unchanged despite sizable capital inflows, and the Bank of Canada regains control over monetary policy.

The tendency toward appreciation of the Canadian dollar resulting from capital inflows adds to the effectiveness of domestic monetary policy through its effects on the balance of trade. Higher Canadian interest rates will attract some money from New York despite exchange risks. The result is upward pressure on the Canadian dollar, which the Bank of Canada should not resist if its restrictive policy is to be fully effective. The appreciation of the Canadian dollar reduces the competitiveness of Canadian products in both foreign and domestic markets, producing a balance-of-trade deficit. The reduced demand for Canadian exports and import substitutes is deflationary and augments the purely domestic effects of a restrictive monetary policy. The same process works in reverse for an expansionary monetary policy. Lower interest rates encourage capital outflows, putting downward pressure on the Canadian dollar in the exchange market. If the central bank does not intervene in the exchange market, the resulting depreciation of the local currency improves the competitiveness of Canadian exports and import substitutes. The resulting balance-of-trade surplus is expansionary, thereby increasing the effectiveness of the monetary policy.

This argument has been put in Keynesian aggregate-demand terms, but almost the same results follow from a monetarist approach. The critical point is that with a fixed exchange rate and with integrated capital markets, the domestic central bank cannot control the money supply. Through the mechanism discussed above, any attempt to enforce a Canadian policy that differs significantly from that prevailing in the United States will simply wash out through the balance of payments. Payments flows will totally frustrate sterilization attempts, producing a Canadian money-supply pattern that is dictated by U.S. interest rates and by the Canadian demand for money balances at these interest rates. With floating exchange rates, the Bank of Canada regains control of the domestic money supply because there are no balance of payments deficits or surpluses to wash out changes in monetary policy. Since, in the monetarist view, the money supply is the only variable of any importance in regulating the economy, once the Bank of Canada regains monetary control it has all the independence and effectiveness it could need or even want.[9]

Disadvantages of Large Exchange-Rate Changes

There is only one problem with this conclusion, but it is a big one. It is the assumption that the Bank of Canada is willing to allow the exchange rate to move at any speed and over any range necessary to adjust fully to monetary-policy shifts. If the Bank of Canada adopts a restrictive stance that produces relatively high interest rates, the result will be a sizable inflow of capital and the possibility of a sharp appreciation of the Canadian dollar. In a relatively open economy, the exchange rate is an extremely important price, and a major appreciation has a number of potentially disruptive effects. It reduces the domestic prices of most, if not all, traded goods, reducing profits and employment opportunities in industries producing such goods. The deflationary effects of an appreciation are not spread evenly across the economy, but are instead concentrated in major traded-goods industries and in regions where these industries are located. Such effects are disruptive and politically unattractive. The

---

[9] For a detailed description of the monetarist view of balance of payments determination in the Canadian context, see Lance Roper and Don E. Roper, "A Monetary Model of Exchange Market Pressure Applied to the Post-War Canadian Experience," *American Economic Review*, September, 1977, pp. 537-48.

appreciation will also impose losses on local holders of foreign assets and on inventories of traded goods. Although the deflationary macro effects of a sharp appreciation may parallel the desires of the central bank, the micro, or distributional, effects are likely to be unpleasant and unpopular.

A depreciation of a currency produces different, and probably more serious, problems for a relatively open economy. A sizable decline in the exchange rate for a currency typically denotes a parallel increase in the domestic prices of imported goods and services, which adds to the rate of inflation. Increases in domestic prices of exported goods will normally be smaller than price increases for imports, but will add further to inflation. If collective-bargaining agreements contain cost-of-living-adjustment clauses, these increases in the domestic prices of imported and exported goods will trigger wage-rate increases and will cause still more inflation. Any government trying to restrain chronic inflationary pressures (it is difficult to think of one that does not fall into this category) will necessarily view a sizable depreciation with great misgivings. The more open the economy, the greater the inflationary impacts of a depreciation, and the more such exchange-rate movements will be resisted.

A depreciation also has painful and almost certainly unpopular income-distribution effects. Increases in the prices of a wide range of traded goods caused by the exchange-rate movement will reduce real incomes for most people by significantly increasing the cost of living. Profits in the traded-goods sector of the economy increase at the expense of reductions in real income for those on fixed incomes or those whose wages do not respond quickly to increases in the cost of living. An event that redistributes income away from widows, retirees, and workers toward profits and land rents in industries producing exports and import substitutes is certain to be unpopular. A study by Richard Cooper indicates that devaluations typically increase the likelihood that a government will fall during the following year.[10] Since sharp declines in floating exchange rates produce the same effects on an economy, they are likely to be equally unpopular. The only advantage of a downward float over a devaluation is that the government does not explicitly choose the new exchange rate and can consequently blame it on impersonal market forces. This seems to be a modest advantage at best.

Large and sudden exchange-rate movements injure major groups within an open economy and will, understandably, be politically unpopular. A central bank cannot ignore these effects when it determines monetary policy; this means that flexible or floating exchange

---

[10] Richard N. Cooper, "Currency Devaluations in Developing Countries," *Princeton Essays in International Finance* 86 (June, 1971): 28-29. The data in this study apply directly only to developing countries, but the same effects occur in all open economies when the government devalues, so the popularity and political problems should be universal.

rates do not offer the total freedom to the central bank that is argued in theoretical terms. The theory assumes a clear distinction between instruments and goals in policy-making and supposes that the exchange rate is an instrument to be used to reach goals such as an equilibrium in the balance of payments and an increase in the independence and effectiveness of monetary policy. The side effects of major exchange-rate changes discussed above suggest, however, that the exchange rate cannot be viewed solely as an instrument, but that it also has aspects of a goal. It is clear, therefore, that monetary policy cannot be designed without consideration of its likely effects on the exchange market. This means that the adoption of a flexible exchange rate may increase the independence of a central bank, but it hardly makes that independence absolute.

Capital-Market Integration and Fiscal Policy

The international integration of capital markets also affects the management of domestic fiscal policy, but the nature of the impact is quite different from that suggested for monetary policy. Under fixed exchange rates, the existence of international capital flows sensitive to interest-rate differentials will tend to increase, rather than to reduce, the effectiveness of fiscal-policy shifts. An expansionary fiscal policy, for example, will increase the level of domestic economic activity, producing a parallel increase in the demand for money. If the central bank refuses to allow the money supply to grow, interest rates will increase, thereby reducing the effectiveness of the original fiscal expansion.[11] If international capital flows respond to the increase in interest rates, however, large capital inflows will produce a balance of payments surplus that will increase the money supply. If capital flows are sensitive to even small interest-rate differentials, the resulting balance of payments surplus should increase the money supply enough to almost return domestic interest rates to their original level. Under these circumstances, the effectiveness of domestic fiscal policy is enhanced by capital flows that do not require significant increases in domestic interest rates.

If capital flows were not sensitive to interest rates, however, shifts in the balance of payments would have a very different impact on the effectiveness of fiscal policy. If the balance of trade is sensitive to changes in aggregate demand because imports rise with domestic incomes but capital flows are unresponsive to interest rates, then an expansionary fiscal policy that increases domestic economic activity will cause a deterioration of the balance of trade. This worsening of the trade account will push the balance of payments into deficit, causing, in turn, a reduction of the domestic

---

[11] Ronald I. McKinnon and Wallace E. Oates, "The Implications of International Economic Integration for Monetary, Fiscal, and Exchange Rate Policy," *Princeton Studies in International Finance* 16 (1969).

money supply as the central bank sells foreign-exchange reserves and absorbs its own currency. In this case the prospects for a successful fiscal policy are quite poor unless the central bank offsets this monetary contraction and precludes any increase in interest rates. If capital-market integration does not exist, but imports — and hence the balance of trade — are sensitive to shifts in domestic income, a world of fixed exchange rates means that fiscal policy can succeed only with the cooperation of the central bank. Expansionary fiscal policy must be accompanied by an increase in the money supply sufficient to avoid any increase in interest rates, and vice versa. If capital flows are highly sensitive to interest-rate shifts, however, the effectiveness of fiscal policy is greatly enhanced by a fixed exchange rate. In this case, an expansionary fiscal policy will produce only a slight increase in interest rates before capital inflows cause a balance of payments surplus that increases the money supply. Since there is only a slight increase in interest rates, the original purpose of the expansionary fiscal policy is not impeded.

In a world of flexible or floating exchange rates, however, these conclusions are reversed. The close integration of capital markets reduces the effectiveness of fiscal policy, and vice versa. An expansionary fiscal policy, for example, that increases domestic economic activity — and hence the demand for money — will cause an increase in interest rates that will attract capital inflows. With flexible exchange rates, however, these capital inflows will cause an appreciation of the local currency rather than a payments surplus. The appreciation worsens the trade account, thereby reducing aggregate demand and offsetting, at least in part, the original expansionary effect of the fiscal-policy shift. Unless the central bank is prepared to cooperate with fiscal-policy changes by adjusting the money supply sufficiently to avoid significant interest-rate shifts that affect the capital account — and hence the exchange rate — the prospects for an effective fiscal policy are not good. In the case of an expansionary fiscal shift, the central bank would have to increase the money supply by enough to avoid an increase in domestic interest rates. This would produce no additional capital inflows, no appreciation of the currency, and no worsening of the trade account.

If capital markets are not closely integrated, however, the adoption of a flexible exchange rate may enhance the effectiveness of fiscal policy.[12] If the current account is more sensitive than the capital account to changes in domestic economic activity, an expansionary fiscal shift will cause a depreciation of the currency, thereby adding to the expansionary impact of the policy change. As an expansionary fiscal shift increases domestic output and incomes, a

---

[12]J. L. Carr, G. V. Jump, and J. A. Sawyer, "The Operation of the Canadian Economy under Fixed and Flexible Exchange Rates: Simulation Results from the TRACE Model," *Canadian Journal of Economics*, February, 1976, pp. 113-15.

parallel increase in the demand for imports will cause a deterioration of the trade balance. This will produce a depreciation of the local currency, which, in turn, causes a recovery of the current account. If the current account is more responsive than the capital account to changes in economic activity (and to the resulting changes in the demand for money), the movement of the exchange rate following a fiscal-policy change will improve rather than hinder its effectiveness. However, if capital flows are more sensitive, the exchange rate moves in the opposite direction, and fiscal policy is made less effective by the adoption of a floating exchange rate.

Theory provides no firm conclusion as to which effect will dominate. If capital markets are closely integrated and capital flows are very sensitive to interest-rate differentials, an expansionary fiscal policy will cause an appreciation of the local currency — and one can conclude that flexible exchange rates reduce the effectiveness of fiscal policy. If, however, imports are very sensitive to income changes and capital flows are not responsive to interest rates, the same expansionary fiscal shift will cause a depreciation of the currency. One can then conclude that flexible exchange rates enhance the effectiveness of fiscal policy. This is a purely empirical question, and the results depend on the particular characteristics of an economy and its international sector. The more integrated capital markets are, however, the more effective fiscal policy becomes with fixed exchange rates, and the less effective it becomes when floating exchange rates are adopted.

3

The Canadian-U.S. Financial Relationship

This chapter attempts to relate the theory presented in the previous pages to the current relationship between Canadian and U.S. capital markets. Limitations of time, space, and data make it impossible to deal with all the issues raised in the previous chapter, so the following discussion will necessarily be selective. The choice of topics to be covered is largely based on the availability of relevant information, and some emphasis is given to the results of a questionnaire sent to financial-market participants in both countries (see Appendix B). The purpose of the questionnaire responses and of the accompanying statistical discussion is to suggest how and, more important, why the current relationship between the financial markets of Canada and the United States has developed.

Net Capital Flows into Canada

General Overview

As noted in Chapter 2, Canada's dependence on foreign capital can be viewed either in terms of net flows of funds into the country (the capital-account surplus minus any increases in Canada's foreign-exchange reserves) or in terms of the inflows of real resources (Canada's current-account deficit) that make domestic investment in excess of domestic savings possible. These two methods of measuring capital inflows must produce the same result if the balance of payments accounts are accurate. In this discussion Canada's current-account deficit will be used as the measure of net capital inflows. This approach has been adopted because it makes the statistical presentation simpler and because it is the current-account deficit that provides real resources for additional domestic investment. Since the purpose of bringing in external capital is precisely to be able to maintain higher levels of domestic investment than the domestic-savings rate would otherwise allow, viewing Canada's dependence on foreign capital in terms of the current-account deficit is not unreasonable.

An important source of net flows of resources into Canada is not included in published current-account data; an adjustment is therefore

41

necessary. When a foreign-owned firm earns after-tax profits in Canada that are not paid out as dividends but are instead reinvested in the Canadian firm, the resulting flow of additional capital to Canada is not reflected in published statistics. The economic reality is that the foreign parent firm has earned profits in Canada, which should be reflected as a debit in Canada's current account, and re-invested these profits in Canada, which should be a credit in the capital account. Since neither the current nor the capital accounts in Canada's published statistics reflect this process, Canada's current-account deficits and capital inflows are systematically understated. (It should be noted that this problem is not unique to Canada; it is common in published balance of payments data for most, if not all, countries.) Any measure of net flows of capital into Canada should include reinvested profits; and in the discussion and tables that follow, this has been taken into account. Net reinvested earnings (foreign reinvested earnings in Canada minus Canadian reinvested earnings abroad) have been added to Canada's published current-account deficits to make this adjustment. The volume of these reinvested profits reported by Statistics Canada has often been quite large, particularly in recent years; the result of this adjustment has been to increase significantly the measured net flow of capital into Canada.

During the 1950-77 period Canada ran a cumulative current-account deficit (adjusted for net retained earnings) of almost $51 billion. During the same period net investment in the Canadian economy was about $239 billion, so foreign resources provided the equivalent of about 21 percent of the increase in the Canadian capital stock.[1] In the private sector of the economy, total net investment during this period was about $165 billion, so the cumulative current-account deficit represented about 31 percent of that investment total. Foreign capital has thus provided an important, but not dominant, part of the resources for Canadian investment over the past twenty-seven years.

As can be seen in Chart 1, the importance of foreign resources in Canadian investment has varied rather sharply from year to year.[2] Canada's current-account deficit represented only about 16 percent of the resources available for total investment during the 1950-54 period, but this figure rose to almost 35 percent during the 1955-59 investment boom in Canada's resource sector. From this

---

[1] Since depreciation data are not available for the public capital stock, gross investment is used in reporting government investment. Net investment data are used for the private sector. The lack of a deduction for depreciation of publicly owned capital means that the data in this study slightly overestimate the actual growth of the Canadian capital stock.

[2] In this study statistical material is, for the most part, presented graphically in the main text, with numerical tables in a separate appendix at the end of the document. For appropriate appendix references, see the sources at the bottom of each chart.

43

CHART 1

Canadian Current Account, Including Retained Earnings, 1950-77

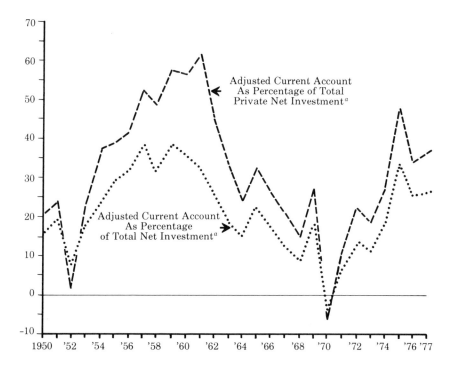

a "Negative" represents current-account surplus (which is a proxy for a capital outflow).

Sources: See Appendix Table A.1.

high point the level of Canadian dependence on foreign capital declined fairly steadily through the early 1970s. In the 1960-64 period the equivalent of 25 percent of the resources for Canadian net investment came from capital inflows, but this figure fell to 17 percent in 1965-69 and to 12 percent in 1970-74. In 1970 Canada actually had a small current-account surplus that temporarily reversed its dependence on foreign capital. But this surplus was followed by a serious deterioration of Canada's current account in the mid-1970s. In 1975 Canada had an adjusted current-account deficit of $7.1 billion, equivalent to about 33 percent of Canada's net investment for that year. During 1976 the adjusted current-account deficit fell slightly, to $6.4 billion, or the equivalent of 25 percent of total net investment. The 1977 deficit was $6.5 billion, or 26 percent of total net investment. The deficits in 1975-77 were the largest of the 1950-77 period and represented the highest ratio to Canadian net investment since 1961.

The extent of Canada's dependence on foreign capital declined significantly and rather steadily from the late 1950s to the early 1970s, which is what the historical view of the role of foreign capital in the development process, discussed in Chapter 2, would lead one to expect. According to this view, as the Canadian economy develops and matures, it ought to require less foreign capital to maintain a given growth rate and should eventually be able to finance all its domestic investment needs and perhaps even become a net capital exporter. The experience through the early 1970s almost exactly matched this model and should have been very encouraging to those Canadians who want their country to become more independent both of U.S. capital and of other U.S. influences. The experience of the mid-1970s, however, must be disquieting both to Canadian nationalists and to others who think that the Canadian economy should by now have reached a stage of economic maturity in financing its own growth. It may be that the recent experience is merely an aberration, soon to be reversed, from the downward trend in Canada's dependence on foreign capital. It is also possible, however, that some combination of circumstances and government policies really has returned the Canadian economy to a level of dependence on foreign resources that was widely thought to have passed into history.

Causes of the 1974-77 Canadian Current-Account Deterioration

Although there were undoubtedly a number of related reasons for this shift, one major factor is apparent in the data for government borrowing. During the 1974-77 period, when the largest current-account deficits were recorded, the Canadian public sector borrowed an average of $12.4 billion per year in new funds — six times the average borrowing level of the previous twenty-four years and more than twice the highest level in those years. Even in the relatively inflationary 1970-73 period, the public sector borrowed an average of only $4.1 billion, which is about one-third as high as the average level for 1974-76. It seems clear that, during 1974-76, the Canadian public sector went on something of a spending spree that was not accompanied by sufficient tax-rate or revenue increases, resulting in a massive increase in the public sector deficit and, subsequently, in foreign-borrowing requirements.

When the public sector borrows massive sums and the central bank is unwilling to provide a parallel acceleration of the rate of growth of the money supply, the predictable result is a sharp tightening of credit markets that pushes private borrowers into foreign capital markets. Given a flexible exchange rate, the resulting capital inflows cause an appreciation of the local currency and an enlarged

CHART 2

Canadian Public Borrowing, All Currencies, 1950-77
(million Canadian dollars)

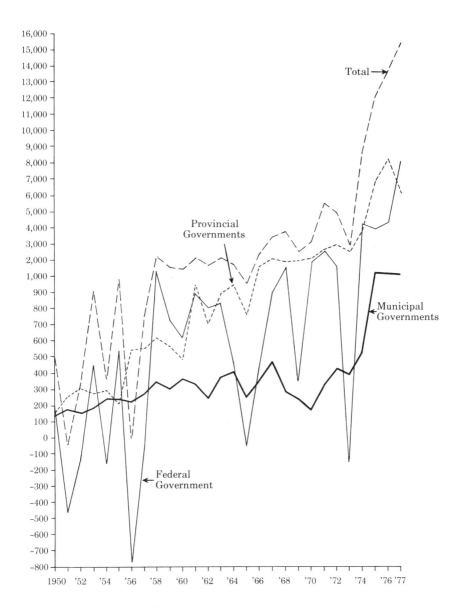

Sources: See Appendix Table A.2.

current-account deficit. When the public sector also borrows large sums abroad, as was the case for Canada in 1974-77, the result is an even larger capital inflow, a further appreciation of the currency, and a larger current-account deficit.

The recent increase in Canada's dependence on foreign capital was the predictable result of government decisions to run large budget deficits. The combination of a flexible exchange rate and integrated international capital markets quickly translates such decisions into an overvalued local currency and a large current-account deficit. The large public sector borrowing requirements of 1974-76 were caused by at least three factors: (1) a major expansion of federal social-welfare programs costing considerably more than anticipated, (2) a bunching of major capital expenditures by provincial hydro authorities and other public enterprises, and (3) an explicit decision by the federal government to use an expansionary fiscal policy in an attempt to avoid the recession that affected the United States and other industrial countries during that period. The problem is that the expansionary effects of Canadian fiscal policy were at least partially offset by the deflationary effects of the resulting current-account deficits.

This raises the question of why the Canadian government did not decide to avoid the U.S.-European recession by simply allowing the Canadian dollar to depreciate as foreign demand for Canadian goods declined, thus maintaining Canada's previous current-account position and avoiding any significant transmission of the business cycle through the trade balance. Whatever additional stimulation was required could have been provided by a modest expansion of the Canadian money supply, which would further depreciate the Canadian dollar and improve the current account. A floating exchange rate provides a well-understood source of protection from foreign business cycles, and it may seem a little surprising that Ottawa did not take advantage of it.

The Canadian decision to maintain an expansionary fiscal policy instead was probably the result of at least three problems or doubts. First, the decision of the Trudeau administration to expand social welfare programs and expenditures meant that the size of the federal deficit was not determined solely, or perhaps even primarily, by the macro-economic stabilization needs of the economy. Second, there is considerable question as to just how quickly and how strongly the current account responds to changes in the exchange rate, suggesting that a large depreciation of the Canadian dollar might have been necessary to maintain the Canadian current account in the face of the recession-induced decline in U.S. demand for Canadian exports. Such a decline in the Canadian dollar might have produced large speculative capital flows and fears of temporary instability in the exchange market. Some exchange rate could certainly have been found to protect the Canadian current account (and hence the level of aggregate demand in Canada) from the effects of the U.S. recession, but it might have been a rate that would have represented a sharp and disruptive depreciation from the 98-101¢ range in which the Canadian dollar had been floating since May, 1970.

The final, related problem is that such a depreciation of the Canadian dollar would have worsened an already serious inflationary problem, caused sizable income-distribution effects, and produced major capital losses in some sectors of the economy. As suggested in the previous chapter, large depreciations produce painful and politically unpopular side effects, such as price increases for many traded goods. Food plays a major role in the Canadian consumer price index, and Canada either exports or imports almost every agricultural product imaginable. Depreciation of the Canadian dollar produces rapid increases in food prices, pushing up the consumer price index, which in turn triggers wage increases for workers whose collective-bargaining agreements contain cost-of-living-escalator clauses. The result is even greater inflation. The shifts in the distribution of income and wealth resulting from a sizable currency depreciation are also certain to be unpopular, particularly when it is noted that the largest capital losses would have been imposed on the Canadian public sector. Provincial governments and crown corporations, such as Ontario Hydro, have borrowed massive amounts of money in the United States in recent years. Since these debts are virtually all denominated in U.S. dollars, depreciation of the local currency raises the Canadian-dollar value of the debts. If, for example, Ontario Hydro borrows U.S.$100 million in New York and moves the funds to Canada when the exchange rate is U.S. $1.00 = Can.$1.00, the local currency value of that debt is Can. $100 million. If the Canadian dollar then depreciates to U.S.92¢ before the debt is repaid, the Canadian-dollar value of Ontario Hydro's liability rises to Can.$108.7 million. Unless Ontario Hydro has arranged a hedge in the form of offsetting U.S.-dollar assets, the corporation takes a capital loss of $8.7 million, which must be reflected as an equivalent reduction in its net worth. A few borrowers may have such hedges, but most apparently do not, with the result that any sizable depreciation of the Canadian dollar imposes large capital losses on a wide range of Canadian borrowers, with major elements of the public sector becoming the most prominent losers.

These borrowers were protected by Canadian-government policy until late 1976, but then the situation changed. Canadian interest rates declined significantly, particularly for short maturities, reducing the attraction for massive capital inflows and suggesting a decline in public sector (primarily provincial) borrowing. This decline in interest rates, along with widespread doubts about the short-term prospects for the Canadian economy and the shock effect of the Quebec election in November, 1976, produced a depreciation of the

Canadian dollar from about U.S.$1.02 to roughly U.S.90¢. This decline in the exchange rate, along with the strong recovery of the U.S. economy, produced an improvement in the Canadian trade account during 1977. A continued improvement in Canada's trade account during 1978 should cause the current account to strengthen further, which would mean a parallel reduction in Canada's dependence on foreign capital and a potential return to the trend of the late 1960s and early 1970s.

Alternative Measures of Canada's Dependence on Foreign Capital

Another way of viewing or measuring the extent of Canada's historic reliance on foreign capital is by the amount by which the Canadian savings rate would have to have been increased to maintain historic investment levels without external resources. The Canadian current-account deficit as a percentage of GNP represents this measure of dependence because, if Canadian consumption could have been reduced (and savings increased) by that proportion of GNP, the current-account deficit could have been eliminated at unchanged GNP and investment levels. This reduction in private and/or public consumption would have required appropriate, but fairly obvious, adjustments in monetary and exchange-rate policies for the level of GNP and investment to be maintained, but this would have been possible if the Canadian economy had saved more and consumed less.

Canada's adjusted current-account deficit averaged 2.55 percent of GNP during the 1950-77 period. This percentage went through a pattern described earlier, rising to 4.55 percent in the 1955-59 period before declining in the 1960s and early 1970s and then rising sharply in 1974-77.

If the proportion of Canadian GNP going into domestic savings had been 2.55 percent higher during this twenty-eight-year period, the economy could have maintained its investment and GNP levels without reliance on net flows of foreign funds. Any combination of reduced private consumption and reduced public expenditure on goods and services that totaled 2.55 percent of GNP would have produced this result. When viewed in these terms, Canada's reliance on foreign capital seems quite small. It appears that a moderate tightening of Canadian fiscal policy, accompanied by an appropriate easing of monetary policy and a depreciation of the Canadian dollar, would have eliminated this dependence.

Another method of viewing Canada's reliance on foreign capital is through the often-asked question of how much less economic growth would have occurred in Canada if historic domestic savings rates had been maintained and if no net inflows of capital had occurred. Put in other terms, what would have been the effect on Canada's economic growth during this twenty-eight-year period of a

CHART 3

Adjusted Current Account
As Percentage of Canadian GNP, 1950-77^a

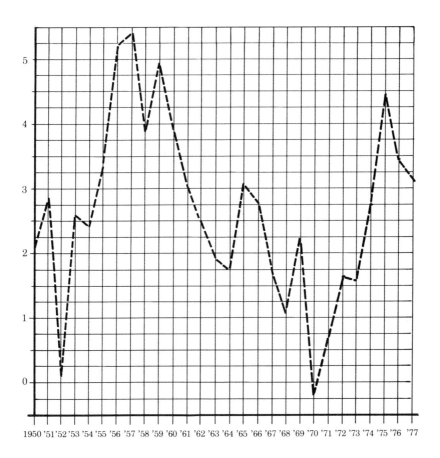

1950 '51 '52 '53 '54 '55 '56 '57 '58 '59 '60 '61 '62 '63 '64 '65 '66 '67 '68 '69 '70 '71 '72 '73 '74 '75 '76 '77

^{a}"Negative" represents current-account surplus (which is a proxy for a capital outflow).

Sources: See Appendix Table A.1.

reduction in the level of domestic investment equal to Canada's adjusted current-account deficit? If the Canadian economy could invest only what it actually saved during this period, what would have been the cost in terms of lost economic growth?

Unfortunately, this question is far easier to formulate than to answer — in fact, so many problems exist in estimating the net effect of foreign capital on the Canadian economy that no precise and dependable answer is possible.

There are at least three major problems in measuring the role of foreign capital in Canada's economic growth: (1) the need for simplifying assumptions about the substitutability of capital for labor and for other factors of production in the aggregate production function; (2) inadequate knowledge about the extent to which foreign technology and access to foreign markets are made available to Canada in a package including foreign capital in the form of direct investment; and (3) the need to sort out the impact of job opportunities created by foreign investment on the rate of immigration into Canada.

The problem of the nature of the production function can perhaps best be seen by considering two extreme assumptions about the substitutability of labor for capital. If one assumes a fixed capital/output ratio, which means a fixed-coefficient production function and no factor-substitution possibilities, it is easy to conclude that foreign capital has been very important to the Canadian economy. Since the equivalent of either 20 or 30 percent of all productive investment (depending on whether one views public investment as productive) in Canada since 1950 has been financed with foreign funds and resources, a fixed capital/output ratio means that either 20 or 30 percent of all Canadian real economic growth since 1950 would not have occurred without foreign capital. Since Canadian real GNP has increased by more than 300 percent since 1950, the role of foreign capital in the current level of Canadian output is obviously rather large under this assumption. The problem is that the assumption of a fixed capital/output ratio is not realistic beyond the very short run, so one must allow for the fact that less than 20 or 30 percent of Canadian growth would actually have been lost without foreign capital.

The question is how much less. An equally extreme assumption would be that labor and other factors of production are infinitely substitutable for capital, so that only the marginal product of capital would be lost if foreign resources had been unavailable. This is the approach used by Edward Dennison in estimating sources of U.S. economic growth and adapted by Thomas Powrie in his first attempt at measuring the role of foreign capital in Canadian economic growth. This assumption means that a reduction of the Canadian capital stock by $51 billion (Canada's cumulative adjusted current-account deficit since 1950) would have no effect on the productivity of Canadian labor and other factors of production and produces the predictable result that foreign capital has been of very little importance to Canadian economic growth. In his study Powrie suggested that only two-tenths to three-tenths of one percent of annual economic growth would have been lost without foreign capital.[3] The obvious problem is that the assumption of perfect factor substitutability is as unrealistic as the assumption of a fixed capital/output ratio, so the results are equally suspect.

Powrie recently published another study of the role of foreign capital in Canadian economic growth.[4] This newer effort, widely discussed in the Canadian press, includes an estimate of an aggregative production function for Canada that is used to estimate the effect on Canadian GNP of withdrawing all the foreign capital that came into the country between 1950 and 1976. Powrie reaches conclusions very similar to those of his earlier study — namely, that foreign capital has played a very small role in Canadian economic growth.

There are, however, a number of problems with the methodology of this study that leave its conclusions in considerable doubt. First, the Cobb-Douglas production function that is used constrains the elasticity of factor substitution to unity. It is entirely possible that the actual elasticity is considerably less than one, particularly in the short run, and hence that Powrie has underestimated the cost to Canada of doing without recent inflows of foreign capital.[5] Since techniques exist for measuring the elasticity of substitution when estimating a production function, it is a little surprising that Powrie used the rather dated Cobb-Douglas approach, which simply assumes a unitary elasticity. Powrie's method of dealing with technical change presents another problem. He quite reasonably assumes that technical improvements are embodied in capital, but erroneously assumes that all capital is equal in its technical contribution. If foreign capital finances about 20 percent of all investment in Canada, then under his assumption, only 20 percent of Canada's technical progress would be lost if this capital were withdrawn. This would suggest that a direct investment in Canada by a multinational firm such as IBM has the same technical impact as the construction of locally financed houses. That is very unlikely, and it seems more reasonable to expect that foreign direct investments by multinational firms provide far more technical growth to Canada than their share of total dollar investment would

[3] T. L. Powrie, "What Does Foreign Capital Add?," *The Canadian Forum*, January-February, 1972, pp. 34-37.

[4] T. L. Powrie (with the assistance of M. A. Gormley), *The Contribution of Foreign Capital to Canadian Economic Growth* (Edmonton: Mel Hurtig, 1977).

[5] A new study by Joseph Schaafsma of the University of Victoria suggests that the elasticity of substitution in Canadian manufacturing is in the range of .63 to .71. He also cites other studies, the majority of which suggest that this elasticity is less than one. These conclusions strongly suggest that Powrie's assumption of a unitary elasticity is in error and results in an underestimation of the importance of foreign capital to Canadian economic growth. (Joseph Schaafsma, "On Estimating the Time Structure of Capital-Labor Substitution in the Manufacturing Sector: A Model Applied to 1949-1972 Canadian Data," *Southern Economic Journal*, April, 1978, pp. 740-52.)

suggest. A $10 million direct-investment undertaking in Canada by Xerox or IBM would certainly appear to have more technical impact than the construction of a $10 million shopping center, but Powrie's approach does not allow for this difference and therefore underestimates the importance of foreign capital in Canadian growth. Powrie also does not allow for the likelihood that foreign firms provide otherwise unavailable export possibilities through their marketing knowledge and access to their home markets. A U.S. firm that builds a factory in Canada has a sizable advantage in selling Canadian output to its U.S. customers.

The problem is that there is no way of knowing how important these difficulties are. The direction of the error in Powrie's conclusion is fairly clear, but the size is not.

Rudolph Penner also uses econometric techniques to try to measure the importance of foreign capital in Canada's growth. He concludes that about 20 percent of Canada's recent economic growth would not have occurred without net capital inflows.[6] Another study by Helliwell and Broadbent suggests that, without foreign capital, Canadian real wages would have been 17 percent lower than they are with foreign capital.[7] Unfortunately, these and other estimates are all based on models of production functions that are far from totally reliable.

As noted earlier, the effect of foreign capital on Canada's economic growth is particularly difficult to measure because of the extent to which foreign firms making direct investments in Canada provide technology and foreign markets for Canadian goods that would otherwise be unavailable. In this case the addition to Canadian economic growth is obviously greater than it otherwise would be — the question is how much greater. If direct investment did not occur, internal responses might be expected to limit any negative effect on growth in Canada. Canadian firms might arrange licenses for some of the technology provided by direct investors, or more domestic research and development might occur to develop indigenous technology. The ready availability of foreign technology through direct investment has probably reduced market incentives for the growth of Canadian firms using such licenses or doing their own research.

In order to measure the net effect on Canadian growth of technology provided by foreign investors, one would need to know how the Canadian economy would react to the lack of relatively easy access to this technology. In some industries, such as the computer industry, technology is rarely licensed, and a fully competitive local

---

[6] Rudolph Penner, "The Benefits of Foreign Investment in Canada," *Canadian Journal of Economics and Political Science*, May, 1966, pp. 172-83.

[7] John Helliwell and Jillian Broadbent, "How Much Does Foreign Capital Matter?," *BC Studies*, Spring, 1972, pp. 38-42.

R & D effort might be unlikely; the lack of foreign direct investors might therefore involve serious technological costs to Canada. In other cases, including segments of the electronics-components industry, licensing is common; a wholly domestic Canadian industry might therefore have access to foreign technology via licensing, and the lack of foreign direct investors would not be so damaging. Since there is no way of knowing how this issue might be resolved in the technologically advanced industries in Canada or how much of the loss in foreign technology could be made up by purely Canadian research efforts, there exists no method of measuring the full effects on Canadian economic growth of the inflows of direct-investment capital.

The same conclusion holds for the role of direct investment in increasing access to foreign markets. Although there undoubtedly are cases in which a U.S. firm's advertising and marketing network in the United States or elsewhere makes it easier to sell products that it produces in Canada, it is also true that if such direct investments did not exist, Canadian firms in the same industries might have developed their own marketing systems in the United States and in third countries.

There is obviously some net impact on Canadian economic growth from the technology and market access that direct investors provide along with capital, but it is not at all clear how large that effect is. All that can be said with any certainty is that any estimate of the effect of foreign capital on Canadian economic growth that looks only at the role of homogeneous capital in an aggregative production function will tend to underestimate the net effect of foreign resources.[8]

Capital Flows and Immigration

The discussion thus far has taken the Canadian population and labor force as given and has therefore implicitly assumed that any effect of foreign capital on Canadian GNP would produce an equal effect on Canadian GNP per capita. This ignores immigration and the distinct possibility that increased economic activity and employment opportunities created by foreign investment will attract additional immigrants to Canada. If the increase in the Canadian capital stock were matched by a resulting increase in the labor force, the capital/labor ratio would remain unchanged and the net effect of foreign capital on labor income per worker would be negligible. The capital/land ratio in Canada would rise, so that returns to Canadian

---

[8] The non-financial dimensions of foreign direct investment are being investigated by Steven Globerman for the project of which this study is a part (Steven Globerman, *Canada-U.S. Economic Linkages Through the Direct Investment Process* [Montreal and Washington: C. D. Howe Research Institute and National Planning Association, forthcoming]).

owners of land and other natural resources would also rise (and Ottawa would receive additional tax revenues), but the wage and unemployment rates would remain largely unaffected by capital inflows. This also means that, if Canada simultaneously acted to reduce capital inflows and immigration, the net effects on GNP per capita might be quite small and the effects on the wage and unemployment rates might be negligible.

Research by John Helliwell indicates a close relationship between immigration flows into Canada and the state of fiscal policy and hence of economic activity. Fiscal expansion produces an increase in GNP, which in turn attracts more immigrants. In one simulation, almost 80 percent of the employment effect of expansionary fiscal policy was offset by immigration, leaving a very small effect on the domestic unemployment rate.[9] To the extent that capital inflows are also positively related to economic activity and to the creation of job opportunities, the same process ought to operate, greatly reducing the net effect of capital flows on Canadian wage and unemployment rates.

Since 1956 an average of 37 percent of the increase in the Canadian labor force has been provided by immigrants registered at the time of entry as "entering the labor force." (Since foreign capital has provided considerably less than 37 percent of the growth of Canadian capital stock over the same period, the Canadian capital/labor ratio is now lower than it would have been if there were no capital inflows and no immigrants entering the labor force.) The tremendous immigration rate of workers into Canada has been both a response to capital flows and a force making further capital flows desirable. (In the short run, continued large capital inflows were necessary if jobs were to be provided for a labor force that was growing at a tremendous rate. On a longer-term basis, these capital inflows were necessary to avoid a reduction in the capital/labor ratio caused by the same growth of the labor force and a resulting decline in the wage rate and in per capita GNP.)

While immigration policies are obviously based on factors other than economics, it does appear that Canada's immigration policy over the past two decades has been a major factor in the country's need for foreign capital. If the population and labor force had grown more slowly owing to a less liberal immigration policy, past rates of growth in per capita GNP could have been maintained with less net investment in plant and equipment and with far less foreign capital. Lower rates of immigration would also have discouraged large continuing capital inflows by providing a smaller and less elastic labor

---

[9] John Helliwell, "Trade, Capital Flows, and Immigration As Channels for the Transmission of Stabilization Policies," in Albert Ando, Richard Herring, and Richard Marston, eds., *International Aspects of Stabilization Policies* (Boston: Boston Federal Reserve Bank, 1974), pp. 241-78.

force. High levels of foreign investment would have produced tighter labor markets and higher wage rates in Canada, making further investment less attractive.

As can be seen in Chart 4, a significant decline has occurred in the proportion of the growth of the Canadian labor force accounted for by immigrants during the past decade. This reflects in part the more rapid internal growth of the Canadian labor force as the postwar baby boom began to show up in the labor market, but it may also reflect what is reported to be a considerable tightening of Canadian immigration policies. If lower rates of immigration are maintained when the impact of the postwar baby boom on the labor force is complete, the result will be a sharp reduction in the rate of growth of the Canadian labor force. This would mean that per capita GNP, real wages, and unemployment-rate targets can be maintained with less investment and hence with much less foreign capital.

Financial Intermediation: Two-Directional Capital Flows Between Canada and the United States

In the latter part of Chapter 2 the process of international financial intermediation was discussed from an essentially theoretical perspective. The purpose of this section is to discuss the integration of the Canadian and U.S. capital markets and the forces behind the intermediation process. The question is no longer why net flows of capital from the United States to Canada occur but, instead, why capital simultaneously flows in both directions across the border — that is, why U.S. residents are typically purchasing financial claims on Canada at the same time that Canadians are making purchases of financial assets in the United States.

Capital-Flow Data

Before discussing why financial markets in one country typically act as intermediaries between borrowers and lenders in the other, it may be useful to say something about the volume of these flows between Canada and the United States. As can be seen from Chart 5, there was a large and growing volume of two-directional capital flows in the form of purchases and sales of outstanding securities in the 1950-71 period. Canadians purchased an annual average of $1,257 million in outstanding securities from Americans during this period, while selling an annual average of $1,216 million to Americans.

The volume of two-directional capital flows between Canada and the United States in more recent years is presented in greater detail in Table 1.

In every year shown in this table, U.S. residents made large purchases of newly issued Canadian securities (line 32), while in most years Canadians purchased newly issued U.S. long-term

56

CHART 4

**Immigrants Entering Labor Force As Percentage of
Change in Labor Force, Canada, 1955-77**

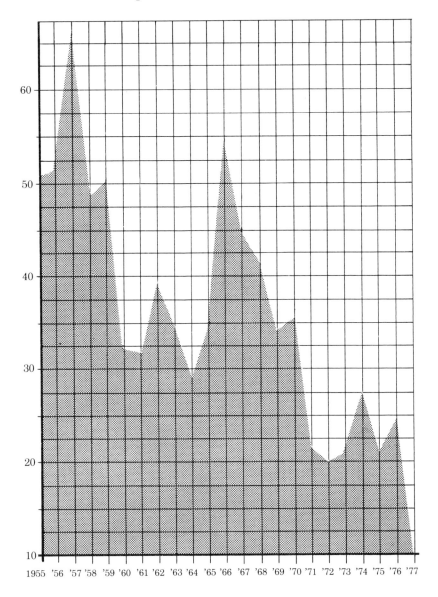

Sources: See Appendix Table A.3.

CHART 5

**Trade in Outstanding Securities Between Canada and
the United States, 1950-71**
(million dollars)

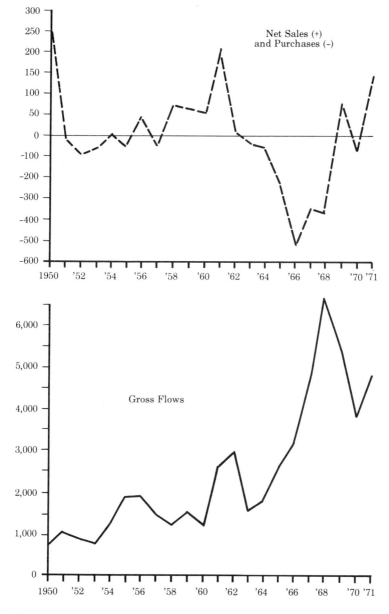

Source: See Appendix Table A.4.

TABLE 1

Capital Account of the Canadian-U.S. Balance of Payments, 1964-77[a]
(million dollars)

Line No.	Item	1964	1965	1966	1967	1968[b]	1969	1970	1971	1972	1973	1974	1975	1976[p]	1977[p]
D	Direct investment:[c]														
21	In Canada	+188	+421	+718	+575	+354	+564	+628	+599	+457	+423	+615	+564	-490	+516
25	Abroad	-35	-24	+87	-72	-108	-287	-258	-122	-149	-453	-482	-454	-234	-497
	Portfolio transactions:														
	Canadian securities:														
30	Outstanding bonds	+38	+21	-72	-63	-67	-27	-71	-74	-5	-29	+16	+38	+20	+44
31	Outstanding stocks	-52	-195	-95	+77	+104	+2	-79	-39	-145	+21	-68	-8	-69	+101
32	New issues	+1,040	+1,200	+1,409	+1,239	+1,391	+1,502	+1,027	+891	+1,007	+990	+1,816	+3,433	+5,609	+2,951
33	Retirements	-300	-330	-456	-301	-376	-382	-395	-649	-458	-428	-504	-666	-706	-562
	Foreign securities:														
35	Outstanding issues	-26	-49	-344	-355	-402	+112	+75	+263	+253	+91	+71	+41	+55	+142
37	New issues	-20	-28	-33	-38	-46	-30	-20	-26	-15	-8	-8	-18	-12	-3
38	Retirements	+5	+5	+6	+8	+16	+7	+6	+6	+19	+11	+8	+7	+42	+8
	Loans and subscriptions — Government of Canada:														
40	Advances	—	—	—	—	—	—	—	—	—	—	—	—	—	—
44	Repayments	—	—	—	—	—	—	—	—	—	—	—	—	—	—
48	Columbia River Treaty	+54	+32	+32	+44	+88	+32	+31	+24	—	+1	—	—	—	—
49	Export credits directly or indirectly at risk of the Government of Canada	+9	—	+25	+7	+8	+3	+1	—	-6	-7	-45	-3	+11	+5
50	Other long-term capital transactions	+42	+21	+116	+196	+189	+173	+44	+4	+101	+307	+153	+336	+351	+80

Code	Item													
E 1	Balance of capital movements in long-term forms	+943	+1,074	+1,393	+1,317	+1,151	+1,669	+989	+877	+1,059	+919	+1,572	+3,270	+4,577	+2,785
D	Resident holdings of short-term funds abroad:														
61	Chartered bank net foreign currency position with non-residents	+310	-519	-517	-197	-464	-477	+55	+1,526	+262	-271	+1,073	+1,485	-611	+881
65	Non-bank holdings of short-term funds abroad	-11	-20	+20	-69	-20	-146	+49	+106	-89	-250	+172	-98	-79	-140
	Non-resident holdings of Canadian:														
71	Dollar deposits	+34	+5	+17	+3	+24	+31	+44	+26	+8	+50	+165	+70	+3	+144
72	Government demand liabilities	-2	+5	-1	-4	+3	+3	-4	—	-1	+2	+9	+1	+27	+147
74	Treasury bills	-16	-15	-1	-4	+1	+44	+69	+37	-113	+1	+42	-5	+286	-121
75	Commercial paper	-11	-208	+3	-67	-62	+190	+128	+36	-52	-22	+73	+232	+18	+33
76	Finance company paper	+196	+13	-33	+7	+10	+2	+35	+76	-17	+167	-108	+153	+146	+270
77	Other short-term paper	—	—	-1	—	—	—	—	—	—	—	—	—	—	—
81	Other finance company obligations	+52	+205	+152	+32	+16	+113	-105	-21	-30	+4	+148	-91	+40	-54
82	Other short-term capital transactions[d]	+141	-103	-112	-467	-931	+1	-224	+81	-169	-271	+86	-87	-181	-651
E 2	Balance of capital movements in short-term forms	+693	-637	-473	-766	-1,423	-239	+47	+1,867	-201	-590	+1,660	+1,660	-351	+509
E 3	Total net capital balance	+1,636	+437	+920	+551	-272	+1,430	+1,036	+2,744	+858	+329	+3,232	+4,930	+4,226	+3,294

TABLE 1 *(cont'd)*

F	Total current and capital account balance	+1	−1,500	−1,110	−791	−1,019	+585	+871	+2,658	+721	−505	+1,702	+120	+241	−640
X	Net errors and omissions														
G	Balance settled by interarea transfers	+27	+1,543	+626	+771	+1,500	−797	+581	−1,598	−430	+76	−1,867	−688	+27	—
J	Allocation of Special Drawing Rights	—	—	—	—	—	—	—	—	—	—	—	—	—	—
K	Net official monetary movements:														
4	Official international reserves	+28	+43	−484	−20	+483	−212	+1,452	+1,060	+291	−429	−165	−568	+268	—
5	Official monetary liabilities	—	—	—	—	−2	—	—	—	—	—	—	—	—	—
6	Net official monetary movements	+28	+43	−484	−20	+481	−212	+1,452	+1,060	+291	−429	−165	−568	+268	—

p = preliminary

[a] A minus sign in accounts D and E indicates an outflow of capital from Canada and represents an increase in holdings of assets abroad or a reduction in liabilities to non-residents.

[b] After first quarter, 1968, transactions in non-monetary gold have been included with merchandise trade.

[c] Excludes undistributed profits.

[d] Includes balancing item representing difference between recorded measures of current, capital, and reserve movements and embodies all unidentified transactions for the years 1964-68.

Sources: Statistics Canada, *Quarterly Estimates of the Canadian Balance of International Payments*, 3rd Quarter, 1973 (Ottawa: Information Canada, 1973), Table 16, pp. 50-51, and 1st Quarter, 1978 (Ottawa, 1978), Table 16, pp. 58-59.

securities in excess of retirements of such securities (lines 37 and 38). In each of these years U.S. firms made large direct investments in Canada, while Canadian firms have made sizable investments in the United States since 1967 (lines 21 and 25). In the 1973-75 period, and again in 1977, Canadian direct investments in the United States were almost as large as flows in the opposite direction. During much of this period Canadians also increased their holdings of short-term claims on the United States (lines 61 and 65) at the same time that Americans increased their holdings of short-term claims on Canada (lines 71, 74, 75, and 81). Other short-term capital transactions (line 82) suggest large continuing flows to the United States.

Despite the sizable two-directional capital flows in both long-term and short-term forms, there has been a fairly consistent pattern in which long-term capital flows predominantly from the United States to Canada, while short-term capital flows in the opposite direction. As can be seen from lines E1 and E2, this pattern held in eight of the fourteen years from 1964 to 1977. In six of these years net flows of both short-term and long-term capital moved in the same direction (into Canada), but only in 1971 and 1974 did short-term inflows exceed long-term inflows. As pointed out in Chapter 2, if the typical pattern is for short-term capital to move south and for long-term capital to flow north, then U.S. capital markets act as intermediaries between Canadian lenders who want to remain relatively liquid and Canadian borrowers looking for longer-term funds.

Relative Yields

The most obvious reason for this pattern is that the Canadian yield curve has typically been considerably steeper than that prevailing in the United States. As shown in Chart 6, until early 1975 a consistent pattern existed in which long-term interest rates exceeded short-term yields in Canada by considerably more than in the United States.

Until 1975, uncovered Canadian and U.S. short-term interest rates were usually quite similar, while a differential of at least one percentage point existed for long-term bond yields. In 1975, however, this pattern changed as the U.S. yield curve became very steep while the Canadian yield curve flattened slightly. U.S. short-term yields fell sharply during this period, but bond interest rates did not decline. In Canada, on the other hand, long-term yields declined in late 1975 and early 1976, while short-term interest rates remained very high. As a result, the usual yield-curve relationship between Canada and the United States was reversed for about two years. During 1977, however, yield relationships in both countries moved toward their normal patterns, and by the end of the year the Canadian yield curve was again steeper than that prevailing in New

62

CHART 6

Canadian and U.S. Long- and Short-Term-Yield Spreads, 1960-77
(percentage points)

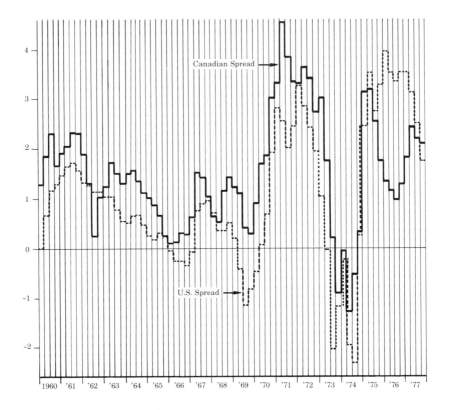

Sources: See Appendix Table A.5.

York. This historic pattern encourages short-term funds to flow south and long-term funds to move north across the border.

Comparisons between the rates of return on equities in Canada and in the United States raise the question of how to measure such yields when part of the profits of typical firms are reinvested in the business. If all the profits of a firm are viewed as being a return to the stockholder, on the assumption that reinvested earnings will be reflected in the price of the stock and hence in the total return to the stockholder, the reciprocal of the price/earnings ratio would be the best estimate of the rate of return to an investor. A stock selling for twenty times earnings then "yields" 5 percent, while one selling for five times earnings has a rate of return of 20 percent. Unfortunately, however, reinvested earnings are often not reflected in the price of a stock, as both Canadian and U.S. investors have learned to their sorrow during the past decade, and the only dependable yield on an equity is the dividend rate. Comparing dividend rates to bond yields is complicated by the fact that bond yields are fixed for the maturity of the bond, while common-stock dividend rates typically increase over time.

Chart 7, prepared by Dr. John Grant of Wood Gundy Limited in Toronto, is based on the assumption of a continuation of past trend rates of growth of dividends for both Canadian and U.S. equities. Current yields on each group of stocks are measured as including the present value of the trend rates of growth of dividends. While some questions might be raised about this approach, including why capital gains are ignored, it is a more conservative and more realistic measure of yields than the reciprocal of the price/earnings ratio and the other usual measures. Capital gains are so uncertain, particularly after the experience of the past decade, that it is probably best to measure current yields based on the assumption of a continuation of the past trend in dividend increases.

As shown in the chart, yields on equities were about equal in the two countries during the mid-1950s, but by the end of the decade Canadian equities had a significantly higher yield. This shift reflected a Canadian stock market that was less buoyant than the U.S. market during the same period. Canadian common-stock prices did not rise as rapidly relative to dividends as did U.S. equity prices. A relatively stable yield differential of almost one percentage point prevailed throughout the 1960s and early 1970s. The differential then fell briefly in early 1975, before rising in late 1975 and 1976 to over two percentage points by the end of the period.

When yield differentials on equities are compared with those prevailing on bonds over this period, as is done in Chart 8, an uneven pattern emerges. From the mid-1950s through the early 1970s, the yield differential on equities rose sporadically relative to the spread on bonds. The bond-yield differential remained at, or just above, one percentage point, while the yield differential on equities increased over the period. In the early 1950s, Canadian equities had yielded considerably less than did U.S. common stocks, meaning that the stock market was more buoyant in Canada than in the United States. By the early 1960s the situation was reversed, and Canadian stocks yielded almost one percentage point more than U.S. stocks; by the early 1970s the yield differential on stocks and bonds was virtually equal, at about one percentage point.

In the mid-1970s the previous pattern returned briefly as differentials on bonds increased sharply. In 1976 a decline in the differential on bonds to 1.7 percent was accompanied by an increase in

CHART 7

Comparison of Expected Real Yields on Canadian and U.S. Equities,[a] 1956-77

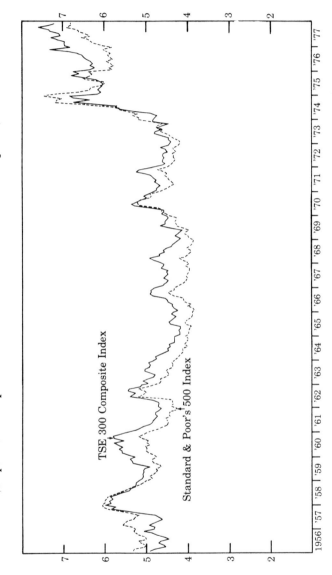

[a]Calculation of expected real yields based on the following assumptions of future growth of dividends per share in constant dollars: for the TSE 300 Composite Index, −0.04 percent in 1978, 2.05 percent in 1979, 4.44 percent in 1980, 5 percent through 1985, and 1.5 percent thereafter in perpetuity; for the Standard & Poor's 500 Index, after 1977, 1.5 percent per year in perpetuity.

Source: Wood Gundy Limited.

CHART 8

Spread in Expected Real Yields Between Canadian and U.S. Securities,[a] 1956-77

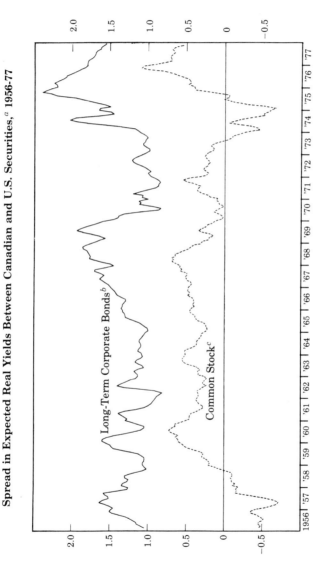

[a]The lines are centered three-month moving averages; therefore, the value for any month is the average of the yield spreads for that month, the preceding month, and the following month.
[b]McLeod Young and Weir 10 industrial bonds average and Moody's AAA corporates.
[c]TSE 300 Composite Index and Standard & Poor's 500 Index.

Source: Wood Gundy Limited.

the differential on common stocks, producing a temporary reversal of the previous pattern. The decline in the Canadian stock market that produced the increase in yields was caused by temporary investor reactions to the 1976 Quebec election, however, and was reversed early in 1977.

In general, however, the trend in relative yields on stocks and bonds in the two countries is reasonably clear. Canadian yields on equities have shown a slight upward trend relative to those prevailing in the United States, while there has been no such trend in relative bond yields. This suggests that Canadian investors may have moved slightly away from equities and toward bonds in comparison to investors in the United States. It appears that increasingly higher yields have become necessary to induce Canadians to hold equities than are necessary in the United States. Since there has been no major shift in relative bond yields, it also appears that Canadian investors have increased their preference for bonds relative to equities when compared to investors in the United States. To the extent that common stocks can be described as riskier than bonds, this shift indicates a growing relative willingness to bear risks in the United States compared to Canada. It may also, however, reflect differing market appraisals in the two countries as to the prospects for domestic corporate profits or changes in the relative political or taxation climate. The Quebec election, for example, clearly dominated the Canadian results for late 1976, producing a decline in the Canadian stock market, which significantly increased yields.

Some Determinants of the Pattern of Canadian-U.S. Financial Intermediation: Questionnaire Replies and Other Evidence

In the previous section recent historical data were used to reach two basic conclusions.

• First, a considerable degree of integration of the Canadian and U.S. capital markets exists, which produces a fairly consistent pattern of two-directional capital flows between the two countries. Although Canadian and U.S. investors are often purchasing similar claims on each other at the same time, the typical pattern of flows between the two countries is for short-term funds to move from Canada to the United States and for somewhat larger volumes of long-term funds to flow in the opposite direction. To a limited degree U.S. capital markets are acting as an intermediary between Canadian lenders who want to hold relatively short-term claims and Canadian borrowers who prefer (or need) considerably longer maturities.

• Second, significant differences in the structure of yields exist between the two countries, which would appear to explain this pattern of capital flows. Until very recently the Canadian yield curve has been considerably steeper than that prevailing in the United

States, which automatically encourages Canadians to lend short-term and borrow long-term in the United States.

Although the relationship between yields on equities in the two countries was also discussed, it is not easy to relate these yields to particular capital flows. Flows of equity funds into portfolio or direct investments abroad do not occur in response to average or typical yields; they occur, rather, in response to particular opportunities in individual industries or firms. In addition, flows of equity funds typically reflect changes in *expected* yields rather than in current yields. If long-term bond yields in Canada rise relative to those prevailing in the United States, for example, investors can be expected to respond, and funds will flow north. A decline in Canadian common-stock prices, however, which raises current yields on equities, will not necessarily attract funds from New York, because expected yields may not have risen. The value of bonds (at least AAA bonds) at maturity is known, so a decline in the price of such assets clearly increases yield to maturity. There is no maturity for equities, and yields in the future are far less certain. As a result, a decline in the price of Canadian equities relative to U.S. equities may simply reflect a decline in expected yields in Canada relative to those in the United States; hence no flow of funds into Canada will occur. The role of highly uncertain expectations and of differing opportunities in particular industries and firms is so important in equities that it is difficult or impossible to relate flows of equity funds to average current yields.

Causes of a Steeper Yield Curve in Canada

Returning to the yield curves for flows of debt capital, the next questions to consider are why Canada has historically had a steeper yield curve and why this pattern has recently been reversed. As suggested earlier, the pattern of steeper yield curves in Canada existed for far too long, and was too consistent, to be explained by the standard "expectations-of-inflation" model. If the Canadian yield curve became steeper for a few months than that prevailing in the United States, one might conclude that investors expected an increase in the rate of inflation and hence in nominal interest rates in Canada relative to those in the United States. When the Canadian yield curve remains consistently steeper than that in the United States for a decade or more while Canadian inflation is not accelerating relative to inflation in the United States, however, it seems clear that differences in expected rates of inflation cannot be a dominant cause, so other explanations must be sought. A search for more permanent or structural determinants of Canada's yield-curve pattern might be undertaken in a number of ways, but this study will be limited to one approach — that is, the presentation and analysis of the opinions of financial-market participants as expressed in questionnaire replies.

Questionnaires were sent to a large number of senior officials of banks and other financial institutions in both countries.[10] Canadian government agencies dealing with capital markets were also included. Private financial institutions were chosen on the basis of their involvement in a variety of Canadian-U.S. capital flows. Written replies to the questionnaire were normally followed up by interviews with a number of officials and analysts in order to gain additional information. The result was a rather sizable body of highly informed opinion on the causes of the pattern of financial integration and intermediation that exists between the two countries. These questionnaire replies cannot be taken as the ultimate answers to the questions raised, if only because the respondents often disagreed, but they do represent the views of people intimately involved in the capital markets of the two countries. In a number of instances, the replies clearly reflected a considerable effort on the part of a number of people within an institution, and a number provided insights and ideas that appeared to be new and potentially very useful.

Although the questionnaire dealt with a number of aspects of the relationship between the financial markets of the two countries, one of the primary topics concerned possible causes of the history of steeper yield curves in Canada than in the United States and of the recent change in that pattern.

The respondents provided no single reason for the prevalence of a steeper yield curve in Canada but rather suggested a number of possible factors. Some causes were, however, far more frequently mentioned and given much greater emphasis than others by the respondents. Of the sixteen replies to this question, seven mentioned (most with great emphasis) the inherent "conservatism" or high preference for liquidity of both individual and institutional investors in Canada. Five of the seven respondents emphasizing this point were Canadian, so this is not merely a case of Americans commenting on their Canadian competitors. This argument was presented by financial institutions on both sides of the border whose representatives were among the most intimately involved in, and best informed about, the financial markets of the two countries.

It was suggested that, for historical or cultural reasons, Canadian investors tend to be more risk-averse than their U.S. counterparts and that they consequently avoid large holdings of long-term, and hence illiquid, assets. U.S. investors were viewed as significantly more willing to take the risks inherent in less liquid portfolios. The result is that there is a relatively greater demand for short-term paper in Canada and for long-term paper in the United States, with a steeper Canadian yield curve necessary to clear the markets. Put another way, the relatively greater preference for

---

[10] A reproduction of the questionnaire can be found in Appendix B of this study.

liquidity among Canadian investors has meant that a significantly steeper yield curve has been necessary to entice them into holding a given proportion of bonds in their portfolios than has been necessary in the United States.

The view that Canadian lenders are more conservative, and thus more eager to maintain liquid portfolios, than their counterparts in the United States is not new; it might be described as the conventional wisdom or common mythology on the subject. (Canadian novelist Robertson Davies recently compared Canadian and U.S. investors in the following manner: "In financial affairs our great defect is an extremity of caution; we seem to have been settled by a more penny-pinching class of person than you were, and we are, on the whole, resistant to feats of financial daring.")[11] An interesting point is that a number of market participants on both sides of the border view this argument not as a myth but as an accurate description of how the Canadian financial system operates. It should be noted that some of the respondents indicated that the degree of this relative Canadian conservatism was declining, both because Canadians were becoming less risk-averse and because loss experiences of the past few years had encouraged U.S. banks to become a bit more conservative. As a result, the capital markets of the two countries are probably becoming more similar in this regard. The end of the legal ceiling on interest rates charged by Canadian banks, which occurred in the late 1960s, encouraged this trend, since chartered banks are now allowed to charge higher interest rates on long-term, and hence less liquid, assets.

The second most frequent response to this question was that the Canadian economy requires far greater relative amounts of long-term capital than does the U.S. economy. Six respondents stressed the importance of growing resource and energy industries in Canada requiring vast amounts of long-term capital. Because of a rapid rate of new family formation and higher building costs caused by a harsh climate, the housing industry, which requires long-term funds, is also relatively more important in Canada than in the United States. To the extent that the growth of the U.S. economy is less dependent on industries requiring long-term funds, one would expect the relatively greater demand for long-term funds in Canada to produce a steeper yield curve even if the asset preferences of investors in the two countries were very similar.

Five respondents suggested that Canadian capital markets are thin and illiquid compared to those in the United States and that this lack of liquidity encourages a steep yield curve. Particular

---

[11]Robertson Davies, "Dark Hamlet with Features of Horatio: Canada's Myths and Realities," paper presented at "20th Century Canadian Culture: A Symposium," conference of the Association for Canadian Studies in the United States, Washington, D.C., April 5, 1977, p. 7.

emphasis was put on thin, unpredictable, and thus unstable secondary markets for outstanding Canadian assets. This means that a Canadian lender is less confident of being able to sell bonds or other assets quickly and easily if the funds are needed before maturity than is a U.S. investor, which encourages Canadian financial institutions and other lenders to avoid purchasing assets with long maturities unless they are certain that the funds will not be needed in the meantime. The result is an increased demand for short-term assets, a relative scarcity of long-term funds, and a steeper Canadian yield curve. As noted in the preceding chapter, a similar argument holds true for borrowers. To the extent that Canadian capital markets are less liquid and less predictable than those in the United States, borrowers cannot be certain of their ability to roll over maturing debt easily and will therefore try to borrow for the full period for which the funds are needed. The result is an increased relative demand for long-term funds and a steeper Canadian yield curve. This argument was presented in considerable detail by one Canadian respondent and in a more abbreviated form by two other Canadians and by two U.S. financial institutions.

Three of the replies noted that, for a variety of historical and regulatory reasons (such as the lack of an equivalent to the United States' Regulation Q in Canada), commercial banks play a considerably more important role in the Canadian than in the U.S. financial system. Since commercial banks tend to maintain more liquid portfolios than do competing financial institutions such as insurance companies, savings banks, and mutual funds, the greater importance of banks in Canada creates a relatively greater demand for short-term assets and hence a steeper yield curve.

Three other respondents argued that the degree of integration of the Canadian and U.S. capital markets was much closer at short than at long maturities and that short-term interest rates in the two countries were prevented from diverging by arbitrage pressures. (This could be true, of course, only when the Canadian exchange rate is fixed and when forward discounts are consequently small.) Since forward cover is unavailable for long-term investments and since long-term assets are inherently riskier, it was argued that the degree of capital-market integration and hence of arbitrage pressures forcing yields together was much smaller. If short-term yields are forced together by arbitrage while long-term yields are not and if the return to capital in Canada is generally higher than in the United States, the result will be a steeper yield curve in Canada. This argument might explain why the yield curve was steeper in Canada than in the United States between 1962 and 1970, when Canada had a fixed exchange rate, but not why the yield curve was also steeper during most of the 1950s and from 1970 to early 1975, when Canada had a flexible exchange rate. With a floating exchange rate there exists the possibility of forward discounts that will fully offset sizable short-term interest-rate differentials, and arbitrage pressures forcing uncovered short-term yields together are much weaker.

Three questionnaire respondents provided support for the "expectations-of-inflation" approach by suggesting that Canadians habitually expected an acceleration of inflation and a resulting increase in the average level of interest rates. This expectation would encourage investors to avoid holding long-term assets on which capital losses would be taken when interest rates rose, resulting in a steeper Canadian yield curve. Those supporting this argument did not indicate why for so many years Canadians maintained a greater expectation of accelerating inflation than their U.S. counterparts despite the lack of any confirmation of this expectation. It is easy to understand why such expectations might exist for short periods of time, but it is not clear how they could continue for a decade or more when Canadian inflation did not, in fact, accelerate relative to inflation in the United States. Expectations that are not confirmed ought to change unless it is assumed that investors never learn from past experience.

Two Canadian respondents noted that Canadian and U.S. debt-management policies tend to encourage a steeper yield curve in Canada than that prevailing in the United States. The average maturity of federal debt has typically been considerably shorter in the United States than in Canada. Since the U.S. government borrows primarily at shorter maturities, it tends to increase short-term yields relative to long-term yields, while until recently the Canadian government has borrowed primarily at somewhat longer maturities, which has encouraged the opposite result.[12]

Three other arguments were made by individual respondents. First, it was suggested that Regulation Q tends to provide low-cost funds for U.S. thrift institutions, which lend primarily to the housing sector. These low-cost funds, along with FHA funds and regulations, artificially reduce mortgage yields in the United States. This spills over into other long-term asset markets and produces a flatter U.S. yield curve. There is no equivalent of Regulation Q in Canada, and mortgage rates are much higher there than in the United States. Another questionnaire reply suggested that Canadian financial institutions have higher cost structures than those prevailing in the United States and that, consequently, the margin between the short-term interest rates at which such institutions borrow and the long-term yields at which they make loans had to be greater. Finally, it was noted that until June, 1975, there was a withholding

---

[12]The Canadian government issues Canada Savings Bonds, which are cashable on demand. These bonds have recently been sold in large volumes, causing a shortening of the term structure of the Canadian national debt. The provinces and their public enterprises, however, continue to borrow predominantly at long maturities.

tax of 15 percent on all Canadian interest payments to foreigners. Since most Canadians were borrowing long-term funds in the United States, this tax increased the Canadian long-term interest rate necessary to attract U.S. funds. The removal in 1975 of the tax on interest payments on assets of over five years' maturity tended to reduce Canadian long-term yields and may have been a factor in the reversal of the Canadian-U.S. yield-curve relationship that occurred during that year.

Although all these arguments are interesting and potentially useful, the first three received the greatest support from questionnaire respondents. The combination of the relatively greater "conservatism" or preference for liquidity on the part of Canadian investors, the long-term capital intensity of the growing sectors of the Canadian economy, and the problem of thin and relatively illiquid secondary markets in Canada makes it easy to understand why yield curves have been steeper in Canada than in the United States. It also suggests why the United States has typically borrowed short and lent long in Canada. If the relative conservatism of Canadian investors declines, and as Canadian capital markets mature and broaden, these differences will decline, and the yield curves of the two countries can be expected to become more similar.

The 1975-77 Experience

In mid-1975 the past relationship between the yield curves of Canada and the United States was reversed. Although this shift was widely expected to be very brief, it lasted two years before being reversed again in late 1977. During this two-year period the yield curve became extremely steep in the United States, while flattening modestly in Canada. The change in the U.S. yield structure probably resulted primarily from the expectation that the 1975-76 reduction of inflationary pressures and the resulting easing of monetary policy would be temporary. If accelerating inflation and higher interest rates had been expected, U.S. investors would have been encouraged to avoid potential losses on holdings of long-term bonds by remaining as liquid as possible. In such periods a strong demand for short-term paper and a lack of demand for bonds typically produces a steep yield curve.

Canadian interest rates behaved quite differently. Bond yields started down during the latter part of 1975, while short-term interest rates continued to rise. The result was a Canadian yield curve that became somewhat flatter than usual during 1976. The result of these shifts in yields in both countries was a two-year reversal of the typical pattern in which the yield curve is steeper in Canada than in the United States. One unusual aspect of the 1975-77 experience was that short-term yields rose sharply in Canada without encouraging a parallel, or at least a roughly equivalent, increase in long-term rates.

Far fewer responses were given to the question of why this two-year shift occurred than to that asking why the previous pattern had existed. The dominant response was that a combination of very tight money-market conditions in Canada and the expectation that this tightness would be temporary caused this change. As noted earlier, the Canadian business cycle did not coincide with the U.S. experience in the 1974-77 period. The U.S. downturn began in 1974 at a time when the Canadian economy was still growing strongly. The Canadian growth rate declined sharply in 1975, but Canada (unlike the United States) avoided an actual decline in annual output during this period. Canada's inflationary problems, however, were significantly more serious during 1975-76 than those of the United States. A highly expansionary Canadian fiscal policy (or, if not a "policy," at least a result) left the Bank of Canada with the primary responsibility for restraining inflation; the result was very high interest rates. Until the fall of 1975 the Bank of Canada apparently viewed interest rates as the target of monetary policy, and hence presumed that its policy was "tight" because yields were high. That approach changed dramatically following a September, 1975, speech given by Governor Bouey announcing that the Bank was adopting an essentially monetarist framework. The inflationary expectations built into the economy made it impossible to suddenly reduce the rate of growth of the money supply if serious disruption of the economy were to be avoided, so the new Canadian monetarism was to be adopted gradually.[13] Although short-term interest rates continued to rise through early 1976, Canadian bond yields started down by the end of 1975, apparently in response to the Bank of Canada's policy change. The adoption of a monetarist approach may have led investors to expect less inflation and more buoyant capital markets in the near to medium-term future, and this expectation would have encouraged them to move funds toward longer maturities. As a result, the Canadian yield curve flattened slightly in a period when fears of worsening future inflation in the United States were causing a much steeper curve.

One reply suggested that an additional factor was the relatively illiquid state of U.S. corporate balance sheets, which encouraged U.S. firms to avoid short-term bank loans and instead to arrange longer-term financing. The result was a shift in the demand for funds in the United States toward longer maturities and a steeper U.S. yield curve than would otherwise have prevailed. It appears,

---

[13] For a detailed analysis of Canadian monetary policy during this period, see Thomas J. Courchene, *The Strategy of Gradualism: An Analysis of Bank of Canada Policy from Mid-1975 to Mid-1977* (Montreal: C. D. Howe Research Institute, 1977). For a discussion of Canadian monetary policy during the immediately preceding years, see Thomas J. Courchene, *Monetarism and Controls: The Inflation Fighters* (Montreal: C. D. Howe Research Institute, 1976), and Thomas J. Courchene, *Money, Inflation, and the Bank of Canada: An Analysis of Canadian Monetary Policy from 1970 to Early 1975* (Montreal: C. D. Howe Research Institute, 1976).

however, that a combination of relatively easy current monetary policy and the expectation of renewed inflationary pressures and higher future interest rates was the major cause of the steeper U.S. yield curve during this period.

Additional Factors Affecting Yield-Curve Comparisons

The questionnaire also asked what significant differences in yields, other than those based on maturity, existed between the capital markets in the two countries. A number of relatively minor but interesting points emerged in the responses. First, it was noted that Canada does not maintain the U.S. tax exemption for interest income from local government bonds and that, as a result, provincial and municipal bonds carry much higher yields than are common for similar securities in the United States. Also, Canada does not make a practice of subsidizing the flow of funds to the real-estate market through policies such as Regulation Q. Combined with a very heavy demand for new housing, this situation produces much higher mortgage yields in Canada than in the United States. Canadian mortgage borrowers have been willing to pay interest rates of up to 12 percent, despite the fact that they cannot deduct mortgage interest payments from their taxable income.

Another difference between the capital markets of the two countries is that the secondary-reserve requirement for Canadian banks creates a somewhat protected market for Canadian treasury bills. In the United States, treasury bills have no particular legal status and hence bring yields that are not very different from other low-risk money-market instruments. Canadian chartered banks are required to hold a small percentage of their assets in treasury bills as a secondary reserve; the result is that yields on these bills tend to be slightly lower than would otherwise be the case.

As noted earlier, yields on equities have typically been higher in Canada than in the United States, but until recently the yield differential on equities has been somewhat narrower than that prevailing for bonds. Comparisons between returns on equities in the two countries are impossible to make with any precision because of differences in the types of firms being compared. Firms listed on the Toronto Stock Exchange are, on average, considerably smaller than those listed on the New York Stock Exchange. This should tend to make the Canadian firms somewhat riskier, which should, in turn, depress Canadian equity prices, but this may be largely offset by investor perceptions that the growth prospects for the Canadian economy and for Canadian companies are somewhat better than those in the United States. In addition, the Canadian personal-income-tax system treats corporate dividends more favorably than does the U.S. system, so Canada partially avoids the "double taxation" problem widely discussed in the United States. This should tend to increase stock prices and to depress yields in Canada relative to those in the United States. Questionnaire replies were not otherwise particularly enlightening on this point.

Differing Perceptions of Risk

One of the common myths of Canadian-U.S. financial relations is that both individual and institutional investors in the United States are sometimes naive in judging Canadian risks. This argument typically runs along the lines that Canadian bankers and other lenders are both better informed and more hard-eyed in judging the credit-worthiness of potential Canadian borrowers. According to this view, risky Canadian enterprises that cannot secure funds in Toronto or Montreal are often able to borrow in New York. The ability of the Province of Quebec and of Hydro-Québec to borrow more readily in New York than in Canada is sometimes cited as an example of this pattern.

Although there are no data that would prove whether or not this view is accurate, the questionnaire was designed to attempt to find out whether participants in the capital markets of the two countries think that it is true. Quebec's borrowing activities in New York were used as the primary example in this survey, which was completed before the 1976 Quebec election brought a separatist party to power.

As one might expect, there was a rather wide difference of opinion on this question, and some of the replies from both sides of the border are probably based, at least in part, on competitive attitudes toward financial institutions in the other country. Although the replies are interesting and informative, they must be interpreted carefully.

The most frequent single response was not that New York is less informed about risks in Canada, but rather that New York financial institutions are simply less risk-averse than their competitors in Canada. Nine respondents, seven of whom were Canadian, suggested that, for a variety of reasons, U.S. lenders were willing knowingly to take on riskier borrowers (including Quebec) than were Canadian institutions. Some attributed this to more intense competitive pressures in the United States, which forced U.S. banks to seek customers more aggressively than was necessary for Canadian banks. Others suggested that many large Canadian banks had a long history of preferring to lend only to large, well-established firms. One respondent did note, however, that the difference between lending patterns in the two countries was reduced by the 1967 elimination of the ceiling on interest rates charged by Canadian banks, since it then became possible for chartered banks to charge higher interest rates as a risk premium to marginal customers.

A number of other replies presented quite different opinions. Six respondents, five of whom were American (the other was from

Montreal), felt that Toronto lenders were simply prejudiced against Quebec and that, consequently, Quebec had to borrow in New York irrespective of credit-worthiness. Five other replies, four of which were from Canadians, suggested instead that New York lenders were not fully informed about risks in Canada and that Quebec's ability to borrow vast sums in New York was a prime example of this lack of knowledge. (A few Canadian bankers were rather sarcastic about the way U.S. banks investigate loan risks in Canada, and one was a little bitter about a sizable loss taken by his bank when it accepted the advice of a U.S. bank as to the credit-worthiness of a U.S. real estate investment trust that went under shortly after a loan was made.)

To summarize the responses to this point, about half the replies indicated that there was no lack of information in New York and no prejudice in Toronto but instead that U.S. financial institutions were simply less risk-averse than their Canadian competitors. Most of the remaining respondents split evenly between Americans who viewed Toronto bankers as prejudiced against Quebec borrowers and Canadians who viewed New York as less than fully informed about the risks in Quebec and elsewhere in Canada. It would be interesting to know how these proportions would have changed if the survey had been made after the 1976 Quebec election.

Another alternative suggested in two replies is that loans to Quebec are inherently less risky for a large New York bank than they would be for a Canadian institution. If Quebec were to separate, it might abandon its liabilities to Toronto banks, but it would be far less likely to default on debts to New York institutions. Quebec and other foreign borrowers need access to U.S. markets for their goods and to U.S. capital markets for future financing. They may delay payment, but the size of the U.S. market and the importance of New York banks means that ultimately they will pay off their obligations. Banks in Toronto are not in as strong a position to compel repayment and therefore avoid what might become risky foreign loans. This view suggests that countries with the largest import and capital markets have a significant advantage in becoming international banking centers. Foreign borrowers will want to avoid losing future access to markets in such countries, automatically making their loans from these countries less risky. One banker summarized this view by asking: If an independent Quebec tried to abandon its New York loans, where would it sell its newsprint and any surplus electricity that might come from James Bay? Since New York and Quebec presumably understand this argument, New York can safely lend to Quebec, while Toronto banks must be more careful. Finally, one respondent suggested that a long history of financial relations between New York and Quebec encouraged this borrowing pattern, but the reasons for this historical pattern are not clear.

The Effects of Relative Market Size

It has also been argued that many large Canadian borrowers come to New York because they need larger amounts of money than can be raised in a single offering in Canada. Many Canadian borrowers, such as Ontario Hydro and Hydro-Québec, are large by any standards and huge relative to Canadian capital markets. Prudent investment behavior makes it impossible for banks or other financial institutions to concentrate their lending on a small number of borrowers, no matter how sound these borrowers may be. The result is that there may be a maximum size for a single bond issue or a private placement in Canada that is too small for some large borrowers, such as hydro authorities or the largest private corporations.

The questionnaire produced a virtually unanimous response in this case. All those responding to this question indicated that many Canadian borrowers simply must come to New York because of the size of their financing needs relative to the size of Canadian capital markets. For a borrower other than the Canadian government, for whom normal borrowing limits would not apply, $150 million is about the maximum that can be raised in a single public bond issue. Private placements in Canada do not go over $100 million. In New York, however, public offerings of $500 million or more are not uncommon; $1 billion or more have been raised on two separate occasions through private placements in New York; and BP-Sohio once raised $1.7 billion via the same route. One Canadian firm noted that, when a financing package was put together for Churchill Falls a few years ago, $50 million was raised in Canada at the same time that $500 million was raised in New York.

A number of respondents pointed out that the problem is not that Canadian capital markets are small (by standards other than those of New York or London they are large), but that some Canadian borrowers are huge. If, for example, Canada's capital markets were one-tenth as large as those in the United States and if Canadian borrowers were also, on average, one-tenth the size of their counterparts in the United States, there would be no problem of borrowers' being too large for the Canadian market. Canadian capital markets are, in fact, about one-tenth the size of those in New York, but many Canadian borrowers are proportionally much larger. Ontario Hydro, Hydro-Québec, and a number of Canadian private corporations are easily as large as their counterparts in the United States and could not expect to satisfy all their financing needs except in New York or London. For reasons that are not entirely clear, Canada has developed a number of public and private enterprises that are very large even by U.S. standards and absolutely massive relative to the size of the Canadian economy. One respondent suggested lightly that economies of scale are obviously greater in a cold climate.

Competition and Efficiency: Canadian versus U.S. Banks

The role that U.S. capital markets play as an intermediary between Canadian savers and Canadian borrowers has sometimes been attributed to a lack of vigorous competition in Canadian capital markets. It is argued that the small number of large banks and other financial institutions in Canada creates a competitive climate in which high profits and relatively low efficiency levels are possible. High cost and profit levels require a larger margin between the interest rates at which banks and other financial institutions borrow from the public and the interest rates they charge on loans. These wider yield margins make it possible for U.S. banks and other financial intermediaries to compete successfully in Canada by borrowing short-term funds and lending at somewhat longer maturities. According to this line of argument, the typical pattern in which short-term capital flows south and long-term capital flows north is simply a case of U.S. financial intermediaries competing successfully with relatively high-cost Canadian institutions. The market power of Canadian financial intermediaries is limited by this competition in the same way that merchandise imports reduce monopolistic tendencies in domestic manufacturing markets.

It would be impossible in a study of this length to discuss the relative competitiveness and efficiency of all Canadian financial institutions compared to their counterparts in the United States. This section will instead concentrate on commercial banks, both because they are a particularly important part of the Canadian financial system and because information is more readily available for banks than for other institutions in both countries.

According to a recent study by the Economic Council of Canada, Canadian chartered banks accounted for 38 percent of the assets of all private financial institutions in Canada in 1967 and for 43.2 percent in 1974.[14] Commercial banks also provide an example of what appears to be a more highly concentrated market in Canada than in the United States. There are nine banks in Canada, five of which dominate the industry, while there are about 13,000 banks in the United States, hundreds of which are quite large. If the relative efficiency and competitiveness argument is valid, it ought to be apparent in the data for Canadian and U.S. banks.

There are two quite separate issues to be covered in this discussion: first, whether the greater concentration in the Canadian industry made Canadian banks significantly more profitable than U.S. banks and, second, whether there is any evidence that Canadian banks are less efficient than similar institutions in the United States. Unfortunately, it is not clear that the available data can answer these questions definitively, since there are serious problems

---

[14]Economic Council of Canada, *Efficiency and Regulation: A Study of Deposit Institutions* (Ottawa, 1976), p. 7.

in comparing quite different types of institutions. The five dominant banks in Canada have branches throughout the country, while a large proportion of the 13,000 U.S. banks are limited to a single office. If the five large Canadian banks are compared only to the largest U.S. banks, New York banks with very limited branching systems will dominate the U.S. list. As a result, the data that will be presented cannot be taken as conclusive because of the "apples and oranges" nature of some of the comparisons; they ought instead to be considered indicative.

The Economic Council of Canada's study on the efficiency and competitiveness of Canadian banks provides modest but hardly overwhelming support for the argument that Canadian banks are more profitable than their U.S. counterparts. As shown in Table 2, in the 1968-73 period Canadian chartered banks as a group had an after-tax rate of return on equity of 12.9 percent compared to 11.0 percent for all U.S. banks and 9.0 percent for the eight largest U.S. banks.[15] During 1963-67, however, Canadian banks were consistently less profitable than their U.S. counterparts. It is clear from this and other studies of the subject that the 1967 Bank Act stimulated the growth and profitability of Canadian chartered banks. Canadian banking was no more competitive before 1968, but it certainly was less profitable. The considerable legal barriers to entry in Canadian banking mean, however, that the increased profitability brought about by the improved regulatory climate has not resulted in the creation of many new banks.

The margin between the interest rates Canadian banks pay on deposits and what they earn on assets has been somewhat wider than that prevailing for U.S. banks on a pre-tax basis, but the after-tax difference is very small. In the 1968-73 period, the difference between the pre-tax-yield margins was .60 percentage points, while on an after-tax basis it was only .14 percentage points.[16] U.S. banks have tax-free income from state and local bonds that significantly lowers their average tax rate, while there are no such tax-free bonds in Canada, so Canadian banks pay a significantly higher average tax rate. Because of the lack of taxation, yields on U.S. state and local bonds are far lower than those for similar bonds in Canada, reducing the average pre-tax yields on U.S. bank portfolios relative to those prevailing in Canada. As a result, the only meaningful way to compare the yield margins for the two systems is on an after-tax basis. This comparison produces a difference of only .14 percentage points, which suggests that Canadian banks are not significantly more profitable than U.S. banks.

The problem with this conclusion is that it is based on a comparison between nine Canadian banks, five of which dominate the

---

[15]*Ibid.*, p. 42.
[16]*Ibid.*, p. 45.

TABLE 2

After-Tax Rate of Return to Equity for Canadian and U.S. Banks,[a] **1963-73**
(percentages)

Year	Seven Canadian Banks	All U.S. Insured Banks	Eight New York City Banks	Difference Between Canadian and All U.S. Insured Banks	Difference Between Canadian and Eight New York City Banks
1963	6.3	9.9	10.1	-3.6	-3.8
1964	7.4	10.4	10.2	-3.0	-2.8
1965	6.5	10.5	10.8	-4.0	-4.3
1966	9.5	9.8	8.6	-0.3	0.9
1967	10.6	11.1	10.6	-0.5	0.0
1968	14.2	11.3	10.1	2.9	4.1
1969	11.9	12.0	8.0	-0.2	3.8
1970	10.4	10.0	7.6	0.4	2.8
1971	11.4	10.3	8.4	1.1	3.0
1972	14.1	10.9	9.9	3.2	4.2
1973	15.1	11.2	10.2	3.9	4.9
Average, 1963-67	8.1	10.3	10.1	-2.2	-2.0
Average, 1968-73	12.9	11.0	9.0	1.9	3.8

[a]Shareholders' equity includes capital, surplus, and reserves for losses.
Source: Economic Council of Canada, *Efficiency and Regulation: A Study of Deposit Institutions* (Ottawa: Supply and Services Canada, 1976), p. 42.

industry, and a U.S. banking system consisting of 13,000 banks, many of which are tiny. If there are any economies of scale at all in banking, one would expect a Canadian banking system of nine banks to be more efficient than a U.S. system of 13,000 banks. It would be more meaningful to compare Canadian banks to similar institutions operating under a similar branching law in the United States. The big New York banks are not adequate for this comparison because until very recently they could not maintain domestic branches outside New York City, and consequently they typically operated with a few large offices.

Banks in California, however, provide a reasonably close parallel to the Canadian situation. California, with a population comparable to Canada's, has allowed state-wide branching for many years. A few large banks dominate the market by maintaining extensive branching systems that virtually cover the state. If California were geographically as large as Canada and if it had as many small towns (and as cold a climate), the comparison would be quite close.

For the purposes of this study, a sample was developed of four California banks that fit the general Canadian pattern and that are about the same size as the five dominant banks in Canada. The Bank of America was excluded from the sample because it is far larger than any Canadian bank and because it would dominate the sample of California banks. Operating statistics were gathered from the annual reports of the four California banks (Western Bank Corp., Security Pacific, Wells Fargo, and Crocker National) for comparison with similar statistics for the five large Canadian banks. A summary of these statistics for 1970-75 appears in Table 3.

As shown in the top line of the table, total income as a percentage of assets is higher for Canadian than for California banks, so *pre*-tax yield margins are higher in Canada. This reflects in part the lower interest rates on tax-free state and local bonds held by California banks. The quite different tax rates facing the two groups of banks are shown in line 2 of the table. On an after-tax basis, net profit rates of the two groups of banks are quite similar, as can be seen in line 3. The California banks had a slightly higher average profit for the six years studied, but the trend over the period clearly favored the Canadian banks, so that by 1975 the after-tax margins for the two groups of banks were very similar.

Although net profits as a percentage of assets were similar, rates of return on equity were clearly higher in Canada than in California, as shown in line 4. The difference between these two measures of profitability for the two sets of banks results mainly from a higher deposit/capital ratio, and hence a greater leverage, in the Canadian system. There was a fairly clear upward trend in profits as a percentage of equity in the Canadian banks over the six-year period, but no such favorable trend existed for the California

TABLE 3

Performance Comparison of Major Canadian and California Banks, 1970-75

Indicators	Canadian Banks							California Banks						
	1970	1971	1972	1973	1974	1975	Average	1970	1971	1972	1973	1974	1975	Average
Gross income as % of assets	7.85	6.82	6.38	6.96	8.85	8.77	7.61	6.56	5.79	5.51	6.39	8.12	7.50	6.65
Income taxes as % of gross income	5.7	5.9	6.0	7.3	5.5	6.6	6.2	6.2	3.1	3.4	1.9	1.5	2.7	3.1
Net income as % of assets	0.38	0.37	0.39	0.36	0.36	0.45	0.39	0.61	0.49	0.46	0.40	0.36	0.42	0.46
Net income as % of stockholders' equity	11.43	11.21	12.15	12.12	13.41	16.40	12.79	11.06	10.62	10.63	10.81	10.22	10.30	10.61
Staff and other expenses as % of assets	2.49	2.44	2.43	2.25	2.28	2.47	2.39	2.74	2.55	2.43	2.39	3.08	3.03	2.70
Number of employees per mil. $ assets	2.11	1.90	1.71	1.49	1.30	1.21	1.62	1.79	1.56	1.37	1.18	1.12	1.15	1.36
Number of offices per bil. $ assets	132.5	119.3	104.9	88.2	74.5	66.3	79.6	49.9	42.7	39.5	34.7	33.8	33.9	39.1

Sources: Figures have been computed from the annual reports of the banks used in this study, as listed in the text. See Appendix Table A.6 for additional comparisons.

banks. The Canadian banks earned more on equity than the California banks in each of the six years, with the greatest difference occurring in 1975. If market power and profitability are measured through rates of return on equity rather than on assets, the Canadian banks were clearly in a stronger position than were comparable California banks during the first half of the 1970s. Of course, the California banks in the sample had to compete against the Bank of America.

Lines 5, 6, and 7 of Table 3 represent attempts to measure relative costs, and hence relative efficiency, in the two sets of banks. The California banks had slightly higher staff and other operating expenses relative to assets than did the Canadian banks, suggesting greater efficiency in Canada. This difference widened during the five years, as expenses rose faster than assets in California but not in Canada. When one moves to the number of employees per million dollars in assets, however, the results change. For the 1970-75 period the Canadian banks had considerably higher staffing levels, suggesting that the lower overall expense ratio resulted largely from lower salaries in Canadian banking. The trend in employees relative to assets, however, clearly favors the Canadian banks. Declines in the number of employees per million dollars in assets occurred in both sets of banks, but the decline was much sharper in Canada. By 1975 there was only a slight difference, suggesting that by this measure of efficiency the Canadian banks largely caught up with their California counterparts during this six-year period.

The most striking difference in the indicators for the two groups of banks is in the number of offices per billion dollars in assets. It is commonly believed that Canadian banks are overbranched, and line 7 of the table lends some support to this view. In the 1970-75 period the Canadian banks had more than twice as many offices per billion dollars in assets as the California banks. During this period both groups of banks increased their assets considerably faster than they opened new offices, significantly reducing the number of offices per billion dollars in assets. This trend was stronger in Canada than in California, so again there was some convergence between the two groups of banks. Even in 1975, however, the Canadian banks had almost twice as many offices relative to assets as did the California banks. Since the number of employees relative to assets was very similar for the two groups by 1975, the Canadian branches must have had far fewer employees than their California counterparts. The fact that Canada has many more small, isolated towns than California partially explains the greater number of very small branches in the Canadian system. Casual observation suggests, however, that the Canadian banks also have many small branches in large cities and that branches of the same bank are often surprisingly close to each other. One recent visitor from New York commented that "there are so many banking offices in Toronto that there is hardly any space for bars and other important businesses."

In summary, except for some evidence that Canadian banks may be relatively overbranched, there is not much evidence that Canadian banks are less efficient than similar banks in the United States. With regard to profitability as a measure of market power, the after-tax profits of the Canadian banks are not significantly higher than those of the California banks when viewed in terms of a rate of return on assets; but when measured in terms of a rate of return on equity, the Canadian banks clearly are more profitable. In the 1970-75 period the Canadian banks earned an average of just over two percentage points more as a return on equity than did the four California banks. This is in part the result of greater leverage in the Canadian banks, but it also suggests that the entry of new banks has not been much of a threat to the five dominant firms. (This may change if the latest revision of the Bank Act allows foreign banks to enter the Canadian market more easily.) However, it does not appear that the pattern of capital flows between Canada and the United States has been determined or greatly affected by the relative efficiency or profitability of Canadian and U.S. banks.

Regulation As a Cause of Canadian-U.S. Capital Flows

The pattern of capital flows between Canada and the United States is often affected by financial regulations in one or both countries rather than by pure market forces. Capital often moves between the two countries in response to legal requirements, as in the case of insurance companies that must make investments where their policyholder liabilities are located, or in order to avoid the impact of other regulations and laws. Tax laws can bias investment decisions by multinational firms, thereby creating flows of capital that might not otherwise occur.

The single most important example of "regulation-induced" capital-market integration has probably been U.S.-dollar banking in Canada in general and the U.S.-dollar-banking activities of Canadian agencies in New York in particular. Under long-standing Canadian banking practice, U.S.-dollar deposits in Canadian banks have not been subject to Bank of Canada reserve requirements. This creates a significant incentive for Canadian banks to solicit deposits and to make loans in U.S. funds. U.S.-dollar banking has also been unaffected by various formal and informal limits on interest rates paid on deposits or charged on loans, creating an additional incentive for the growth of such operations. In the United States, Canadian and other foreign bank agencies could solicit U.S.-dollar deposits for their head offices without being affected either by U.S. reserve requirements or by Regulation Q. The result was a considerable advantage for Canadian bank agencies in New York in their competition with U.S. banks for deposits. Since these deposits were booked on head offices in Toronto or Montreal, they escaped U.S. regulations; since they were denominated in U.S. dollars, they escaped Canadian regulations. Often this money was lent back to the New York agency by the Canadian head office and then relent to U.S. customers. The results were a two-directional short-term capital flow and a U.S.-dollar banking business carried on by Canadian banks in New York almost totally without regulation. Recently, "voluntary" reserve requirements have been applied to funds lent back from head offices to U.S. agencies above a historic base to reduce the advantages of Canadian banks in New York. U.S. funds solicited in New York, booked on head offices in Canada, and lent directly by head offices to either Canadian or U.S. customers still escape Canadian and U.S. reserve requirements.

The situation described for U.S.-dollar banking in Canada is common in many international banking markets and has strongly encouraged the creation and growth of the Euro-dollar and other offshore banking markets. Most central banks impose reserve requirements and other regulations only on banking done in the local currency. Since local banking activity carried on in any foreign currency is exempted from such regulations, the development of a relatively liberal environment for international capital flows since the 1950s has created a strong incentive for banks both to solicit deposits and to make loans in one or more foreign currencies. The result has been the development of a massive offshore banking business operating almost entirely without regulation. The London Euro-currency market is the largest and best-known example of such foreign-currency banking, but other examples exist in many other countries, with the Asian-dollar market in Singapore being the most recent entrant.

Canadian banks were heavily involved in an exact parallel to Euro-dollar banking years before it became well-established in London, and foreign-currency banking remains a major factor in Canadian banking. U.S.-dollar and other foreign-currency banking is now so well established in Canada that it would probably survive the lack of regulatory encouragement, but there is little doubt that the anomalies of Canadian and U.S. laws, which made it possible to avoid the banking regulations of both countries by carrying on U.S.-dollar banking through Canadian banks and their U.S. agencies, were a major inducement for the creation and growth of this business. Chart 9 indicates the importance of U.S-dollar assets and liabilities to Canadian banking.

Legislation was passed in Washington in September, 1978, that will regulate and otherwise treat foreign banks in the United States like domestic banks.

CHART 9

U.S.-Dollar Assets and Liabilities in Canadian Chartered Banks,
End of Period, 1963-77

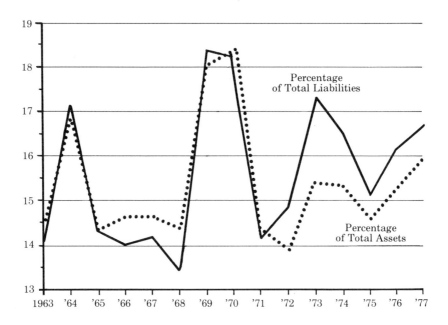

Sources: See Appendix Table A.7.

The Canadian Bank Act is also due for revision, and proposals have been made to allow foreign banks into Canada on a regular, and regulated, basis. A somewhat odd situation has existed since the last revision. U.S. banks cannot operate as banks in Canada, but they can carry on a variety of financial activities through other institutional arrangements, some of which are denied to Canadian banks under the current law. Here again, the pattern of Canadian-U.S. financial integration is determined not solely by market forces, but also by unusual features of the regulatory climate. There is a fair chance that this situation will change after the revision of the Bank Act. U.S. banks may be able to operate as banks in Canada, and Canadian banks may be able to compete with U.S.-owned leasing firms and other "near banks."

The foreign investments of Canadian and U.S. insurance companies represent another example of capital flows induced by regulation rather than by market forces. There is a long history of Canadian insurance companies selling policies in the United States (Sun Life is the prime example, and many Americans are probably unaware that it is Canadian) and of U.S. firms selling policies in Canada. To a considerable degree there is free trade, and therefore one market, for life insurance policies in North America. The regulatory authorities on both sides of the border, however, require that investments be made in each country in proportion to policy liabilities in that jurisdiction. Sun Life must maintain U.S. assets that correspond to its U.S.-policy obligations, and U.S. insurance companies selling policies in Canada must maintain Canadian assets for the same reason. The result is that insurance companies in both countries often move funds across the border in response to changes in policy obligations rather than in response to relative yields.

The U.S. corporate-tax law creates another incentive for such capital flows. Profits earned by Canadian subsidiaries of U.S. firms are taxable in Canada as regular corporate income. When after-tax profits are paid as dividends to the parent firm, U.S. tax laws apply under the current tax treaty; and although a credit is allowed for taxes paid to the Canadian government, some tax liability to the United States typically remains to be paid. If the subsidiary does not pay dividends to its parent firm, however, and instead reinvests the profits in Canada, no U.S. taxes apply.

The result is that U.S. firms with subsidiaries in Canada (and in most other countries) have a clear incentive to keep foreign profits abroad in the subsidiaries where they are earned rather than to allow them to flow back to the parent firm for reinvestment wherever potential profit rates are highest. This is particularly true if the subsidiaries are located in countries such as Canada, where the corporate-tax rate is significantly lower than the 48 percent rate prevailing in the United States. The result is that investment decisions by U.S. and other multinational firms are biased to some degree toward reinvestment where past profits have been earned. Funds are allocated among divisions of the firm not purely on the basis of relative pofitability of potential projects, but in part on the basis of avoiding residual U.S. taxes. As a result, U.S. firms have probably reinvested more in Canada (and in other countries where earlier investments had been made) than pure profitability considerations would warrant. There has been some discussion in Washington of changing the U.S. tax laws to make any residual U.S. tax liability on foreign profits payable when profits are earned rather than when dividends are actually paid to U.S. parent firms. Tax-rate schedules would not be changed, and U.S. tax credits for taxes paid to foreign governments would remain in effect, but the incentive to avoid paying dividends back to U.S. parent firms would be ended. Such a change in U.S. tax law would end one bias in U.S. corporate investment decisions, and its effect on the overall corporate-tax rate could easily be offset with a modest reduction in the current 48 percent marginal rate.

Economic theory has typically viewed international capital flows of all types as being responsive to market forces. The previous paragraphs suggest that, at least in a few cases, Canadian-U.S. capital flows are instead the result of a combination of market forces plus regulations and laws. Canadian and U.S. banking laws are the most striking examples of this phenomenon. Two-directional capital flows and the development of a sizable U.S.-dollar banking business in Canada have developed to a considerable degree as a means of avoiding reserve requirements in both countries and restrictions on deposit interest rates in the United States. There are other examples of "regulation-induced" capital flows, but few are as striking as the U.S.-dollar business done by Canadian banks on both sides of the border.

The Reserve-Currency Role of the U.S. Dollar

The final reason for capital flows between Canada and the United States that does not relate directly to relative interest rates is the reserve-currency role of the U.S. dollar. Canada maintains the vast majority of its foreign-exchange reserves in the form of U.S.-dollar liabilities of the Federal Reserve System and the U.S. government. This means that Canada lends money to the United States whenever these reserves increase. As shown in Chart 10, the resulting flows of capital in and out of Canada are often sizable.

When Canada had a fixed exchange rate, as was the case from 1962 to mid-1970, these flows of capital were simply the residual item in Canada's balance of payments. Canada lent money to the United States by building up foreign-exchange reserves in the form of claims on the U.S. government whenever a payments surplus existed, and vice versa. These capital flows were caused by all the factors that affect Canada's balance of payments position, including interest-rate relationships. In the case of a fixed-exchange-rate system, however, higher interest rates in Canada attracted private flows of capital into that country, pushing the payments accounts into surplus and causing Canada to lend funds back to the United States as foreign-exchange reserves. High Canadian interest rates were thus associated with private capital inflows and official capital outflows in return for foreign-exchange reserves.

When Canada has had a flexible or floating exchange rate, as has now been the case since 1970, the causes of this particular form of capital flow are more complex. In a pure or "clean" float there would be no flows of capital in the form of movements of foreign-exchange reserves because there would be no central-bank intervention in the exchange markets. In the real world of managed, or "dirty," floats, however, foreign-exchange reserves change whenever the central bank chooses to intervene in the exchange market because it wants to determine, or at least influence, the movement of

CHART 10

Canadian Foreign Exchange Reserves, End of Period, 1961-77
(million U.S. dollars)

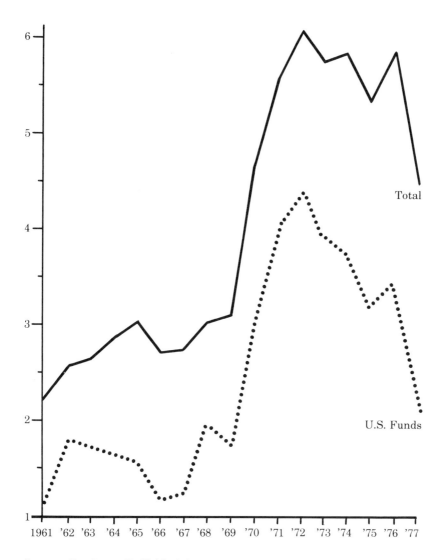

Sources: See Appendix Table A.8.

the exchange rate. This typically means that the central bank re-
sists sharp movements in the exchange rate. An appreciation of the
Canadian dollar encourages the Bank of Canada to purchase U.S.
dollars, thereby adding to Canada's holdings of official claims on the

United States, and vice versa. At least in theory, however, a central bank might become more aggressive in its intervention activities by trying to drive the exchange rate in a desired direction or by precluding any movement in response to a particular market shift.

In the case of a managed or dirty floating exchange rate, capital flows in the form of changes in a country's foreign-exchange reserves obviously have no single cause. They occur whenever a central bank is unhappy with the exchange-rate changes that market forces cause. The determinants of these flows then become all the forces tending to cause changes in the market exchange rate and the factors influencing the central bank's exchange-rate preferences. To the extent that the central bank merely prefers a relatively stable exchange rate, the same forces that would produce a payments surplus in a fixed-exchange-rate world would cause the central bank to purchase foreign exchange and thereby to lend to the reserve-currency country, and vice versa in the case of forces tending to produce a deficit. The Bank of Canada, for example, would purchase U.S. dollars whenever an improving Canadian trade or capital account produced an appreciation of the Canadian dollar and would sell U.S. dollars in the opposite situation. If the central bank's exchange-rate preferences are more complex than a mere desire for a relatively stable market, however, the forces behind capital flows caused by changes in foreign-exchange reserves also become more complicated, but this takes us well beyond the main point of this chapter.

This chapter has discussed the fact that the forces behind capital flows between Canada and the United States, and hence behind the integration of the capital markets of the two countries, are more complex than a mere response to a higher average level of interest rates in Canada. The purpose of the next chapter is to discuss the effect of a flexible or floating exchange rate on the extent and form of Canadian-U.S. capital-market integration and on the degree of independence in Canadian fiscal and monetary policies in light of that integration.

4

Flexible Exchange Rates and Canadian-U.S. Capital-Market Integration

Despite the adoption of floating or flexible exchange rates by many industrial countries in 1973, Canada remains the country with the longest, and probably most successful, experience with this exchange-rate regime (see Chart 11). Canada maintained a flexible-exchange-rate system from 1950 to 1962 and returned to a float in mid-1970, almost two years before other industrialized countries abandoned fixed parities. Since flexible exchange rates were given

CHART 11

The Canadian Dollar, 1940-78[a]
(U.S. cents)

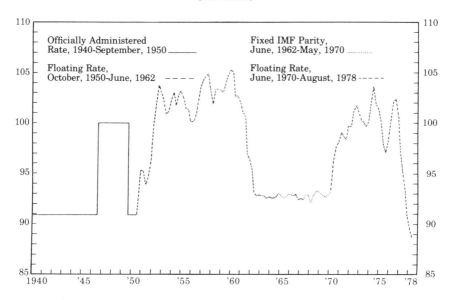

[a]Quarterly averages of noon spot rates.
Source: The Bank of Nova Scotia.

the reluctant blessing of the IMF in Kingston, Jamaica, in January, 1976, this previously radical, or at least unorthodox, system has become a widely accepted norm, and there is now little reason to believe that Canada or the other advanced countries maintaining floating exchange rates will return to fixed parities in the foreseeable future.

The existence of a flexible exchange rate for the Canadian dollar affects, and to some degree complicates, the integration of the capital (and other) markets of Canada and the United States. Two sets of issues are raised by the existence of a flexible exchange rate. The first might be described as the micro-economic impact — that is, how flexible exchange rates affect individual capital- and current-account transactions. Flexible exchange rates have been widely criticized on the grounds that they introduce additional costs and risks in using the exchange market and in carrying on a variety of international transactions. As a result, it has been feared that flexible exchange rates would reduce the volume of international trade and capital transactions and, consequently, reduce the efficiency of the world economy. With regard to the narrower focus of this study, it has been suggested that a floating Canadian dollar will reduce the degree of integration of both commodity and capital markets in Canada and the United States. One of the purposes of this chapter is to attempt to find out whether the current floating exchange rate for the Canadian dollar has significantly inhibited Canadian-U.S. capital-market integration or has had major effects on how commercial and financial transactions between the two countries are carried out.

The second area of impact might be described as the macro effects of floating exchange rates. The combination of a flexible exchange rate and some degree of capital-market integration affects both the independence and the effectiveness of domestic fiscal and monetary policies. The existence of a flexible exchange rate for the Canadian dollar also affects the extent to which business cycles are transmitted from the United States to Canada through balance of payments shifts. The second purpose of this chapter is to review recent attempts to measure these impacts for the Canadian case.

Transactions Costs and Exchange Risks

One of the most commonly suggested disadvantages of floating exchange rates is that constant changes in market rates will create additional risks of loss for foreign-exchange traders in commercial banks, which will in turn force them to widen the bid/asked margins they offer to their customers. This process increases transactions costs to those using the exchange market and presumably discourages international transactions. Both trade and capital flows might be inhibited by such increases in transactions costs, with accompanying efficiency and welfare losses.[1] According to this argument, a

---

[1] An extensive discussion of this argument can be found in Leland Yeager, *Interna-*

foreign-exchange trader who is confident that the rate will not move significantly between the time he takes on a commitment to purchase a currency and the time he can cover his position through an offsetting transaction can quote narrow bid/asked margins without major risk of loss. If the rate is moving constantly, however, any uncovered position that is taken for even a few minutes creates a risk, so the trader will widen his bid/asked margins as an insurance premium. The result is that both commercial enterprises and financial institutions find that the exchange market is more expensive to use and are therefore encouraged to concentrate their activities in domestic markets and to avoid international involvements.

Recent research on this topic presents the interesting conclusion that bid/asked margins did, in fact, widen for a number of currencies, but *not* for the Canadian dollar, after the 1973 adoption of a float. One study actually showed a decline in bid/asked margins for Canada between 1970 and 1975, while another showed an extraordinarily small increase. For all other currencies, increases occurred over the same time periods.[2] Even where increases were reported, however, the total costs were extremely small and would hardly seem to be an impediment to any but the most marginal transactions. In most cases, bid/asked margins of one-tenth to two-tenths of a percentage point were reported, with one-half of a percentage point being the greatest.

Trading Margins

The questionnaire responses obtained for this study strongly support the conclusion that floating exchange rates have not led to a widening of margins for Canadian-dollar/U.S.-dollar trades. Out of eight responses to this question, many of which were from banks very actively engaged in the Toronto and New York markets, four said that the margins may have actually narrowed, particularly for forward transactions, and three said that there had been no change. Only one response suggested an increase, and it was written in a way that indicated it might have been referring to Canadian-dollar/European-currency trades rather than to transactions into

---

tional Monetary Relations: Theory, History, and Policy, 2nd ed. (New York: Harper and Row, 1976), pp. 252-77. Robert Aliber remains a strong supporter of this position (Robert Aliber, "The Firm under Pegged and Floating Exchange Rates," *Scandinavian Journal of Economics* 2 [1976]: 309-22).
[2] Ronald I. McKinnon, "Floating Exchange Rates: The Emperor's New Clothing," cited in Robert Aliber, *op. cit.* See also Norman Fieleke, "Exchange Rate Flexibility and the Efficiency of the Foreign Exchange Market," *International Finance Discussion Paper*, No. 44 (Washington, D.C.: Board of Governors of the Federal Reserve System, 1974), pp. 4-5, and Charles Pigott, Richard Sweeney, and Thomas Willett, "The Uncertainty Effects of Exchange Rate Fluctuations under the Current Float," paper presented at the Conference on Monetary Theory and Policy, Konstanz, West Germany, June, 1975, and at the American Enterprise Institute Conference on Floating Exchange Rates, Washington, D.C., 1976, Table 7.

U.S. dollars. Both published work and the questionnaire responses strongly suggest that there has not been a widening of bid/asked margins between the Canadian and the U.S. dollars. It appears, however, that a widening probably did occur in exchange markets for European currencies, raising the question of why the market for the Canadian dollar performed differently.

Some of the questionnaire responses suggested that the maintenance of, or reduction in, margins in the face of a floating exchange rate resulted from a large increase in the volume of exchange trading, particularly for forward contracts. It was suggested that this increase in volume gave the market more depth and resilience, resulting in narrower margins. Some respondents also indicated that competition among the banks for exchange business became more intense, but it was not suggested why this occurred.

The difference between the experience of the Canadian dollar and that of a number of European currencies probably results from the fact that floating exchange rates are a new phenomenon for Europe and hence for traders of European currencies. There was (and still may be) a learning process going on in which banks widened margins to protect themselves as they slowly became familiar with a very different trading environment. In the case of the Canadian dollar, however, there was nothing new about flexible exchange rates in 1970, and traders on both sides of the border were merely returning to an environment they had come to know well between 1950 and 1962. There was much less uncertainty in the trading rooms of the big Canadian banks when Canada returned to a float in 1970 than in the European banks when European currencies were floated in 1973. As a result, one would expect narrower margins and a more stable market for the Canadian dollar than for European currencies, and that is what happened. It also seems likely that the bid/asked margins will narrow for European currencies as banks on both sides of the Atlantic become more familiar with floating rates; this may already be happening.

The extra risk commonly associated with floating exchange rates results primarily because most importers must pay, within thirty to ninety days, in the exporter's currency. A floating exchange rate presents the possibility that the exporter's currency may appreciate significantly during the thirty- or ninety-day period, imposing increased local currency costs on the importer. If the transaction is invoiced in the importer's currency, the same risk exists but is transferred to the exporter. Similar risks exist for any movement of short-term or long-term capital, leading some critics of flexible exchange rates to suggest that such a system discourages both capital flows and merchandise trade. If both investors and managers of commercial enterprises are presumed to be risk-averse, the possibility of frequent and sizable rate movements provided by a floating-exchange-rate system might be expected to encourage them to emphasize domestic activities and to reduce their international involvements.

Forward Markets

In the case of Canada and the United States, there are a number of answers to this argument, the first of which is that the very active Canadian-dollar/U.S.-dollar forward market provides an obvious way of eliminating exchange risks for periods of up to one year. The existence of a flexible exchange rate ought to encourage importers and others involved in short-term capital flows to make more active use of the forward market. The questionnaire included an inquiry as to whether the use of the forward market had increased significantly since Canada's return to a floating exchange rate in 1970, and the almost universal answer was that it had. Nine respondents, including all but one of the banks deeply involved in the exchange market, reported large increases in the volume of forward transactions after the return to a floating exchange rate, and one Canadian commercial bank said that its forward business had "boomed" since 1970. Some replies suggested that the August, 1971, and early-1973 exchange crises were as important as the 1970 Canadian float in increasing awareness of exchange risks, and hence the use of the forward market, on both sides of the Canadian-U.S. border.

A recent report by the Conference Board indicates that U.S. firms are now making extensive efforts to cover or hedge short-term exchange-rate exposure both through the use of the forward market and through other means.[3] The Franklin National and Herstadt bankruptcies apparently convinced many managers that exchange speculation was an extremely dangerous way to gamble with a company's assets. If what were thought to be sophisticated bankers with long experience in exchange markets could lose that much money, how could managers of industrial enterprises, with little or no direct experience in exchange markets, expect to avoid losing money if they speculated in foreign exchange? Recent changes in U.S. corporate-accounting rules, which require that exchange gains and losses be fully reflected in earnings when they occur rather than deferred through the use of special reserves, provide another reason to avoid speculating, since any losses will now be immediately apparent to stockholders. Both the Conference Board report and the questionnaire replies suggest that there is now a considerably stronger desire to avoid large exposure to exchange losses than existed only a few years ago. The result is considerably heavier use of the forward market and of other hedging techniques.

---

[3] Michael Duerr, *Protecting Corporate Assets under Floating Currencies* (New York: The Conference Board, 1975).

Alternative Hedging Techniques

The alternatives to the use of the forward market as a hedging technique typically involve shifting other balance-sheet items to create an offset to a new exchange risk. If, for example, a U.S. automotive firm buys Can.$10 million in parts from a Canadian firm on ninety-day terms, it can offset the resulting risk by instructing its sales office to invoice the next $10 million in export sales to Canadian customers in Canadian funds. This results in offsetting Canadian-dollar payables and receivables with the same maturity. Canadian importers of U.S. products are not likely to object, since this arrangement relieves them of the necessity of arranging a hedge for a U.S.-dollar account payable. This technique works, however, only if a firm is typically involved in a large number of transactions in both directions across the Canadian border so that offsetting transactions can be found quickly.

Multinational firms can also use shifts in the location of their normal borrowing activities to accomplish the same purpose. If, for example, IBM has a large ninety-day payable in Canadian funds, it can instruct its Canadian subsidiary to reduce its domestic short-term borrowing by that amount and to instead borrow in U.S. dollars from banks in New York. If IBM in the United States has a Canadian-dollar account payable and IBM in Canada has a U.S.-dollar bank loan of the same amount with the same maturity, IBM as a whole does not have any exchange exposure. Many multinationals apparently keep track of all the foreign-exchange assets and liabilities of their various divisions and look for offsets that arise in the normal course of business. They then calculate their net exposure in each currency and either adjust other short-term assets and liabilities or enter the forward market to approximately even up their positions. Changes in invoicing patterns on upcoming export sales or shifts in the currencies in which bank loans are arranged offer obvious alternatives to the forward market for a large firm. As a result, even the reported increase in the volume of forward transactions undoubtedly underestimates by a large margin the amount of hedging of exchange exposure that actually occurs. For small firms, however, that have only a few foreign transactions, virtually all of which are in the same direction, these internal hedging techniques are not available, and the forward market is the obvious way to avoid exchange exposure. If, for example, a U.S. firm imports regularly from Canada but never exports to Canada and has no subsidiaries or other financial relationships there, the forward market is the only apparent way to hedge its Canadian-dollar accounts payable.

For long-term capital flows, where forward cover and other short-term hedging techniques are irrelevant, uncovered exchange risk exists, but it is not obvious that this risk is necessarily greater with a flexible-exchange-rate system than with the "fixed" parities of the Bretton Woods system. There is no such thing as a really fixed parity, and the frequent and sometimes unexpected parity changes of the 1960s and early 1970s created sizable capital losses for many investors. The French franc was devalued three times between 1957 and 1970, so the fact that France maintained a fixed parity did little to protect foreign investors in long-term French assets. The deutsche mark (DM) was revalued twice during the same period, and other currencies also moved from time to time. Unless the world returns to the rigidly fixed exchange rates of the pre-1914 gold standard (the likelihood of which is zero), exchange risk will always exist on long-term capital flows, and the only question is whether parities will be moved occasionally by rather large amounts or whether smaller exchange-rate changes will occur continuously.

Flexible Exchanges Rates and the Volume of Foreign Trade and Investment

If the additional risks and transactions costs attributed by some observers to flexible exchange rates are of any real importance, that fact ought to be apparent in data for international trade and capital flows. The adoption of floating exchange rates ought to cause a significant decline in the volume of trade and capital flows, or at least a sharp decline in the rate of growth of these transactions. There is very little evidence of any such decline, and it appears instead that the purported restrictive effects of flexible exchange rates on international transactions are very modest, and probably non-existent.

Trade Impacts

As shown in Chart 12, there was no significant decline in Canada's role in world trade when Canada adopted a floating exchange rate in 1950. Canada's trade grew about as quickly as the total volume of world trade in the 1950s and did not rise sharply when a fixed parity was adopted in May, 1962.

This comparison is difficult to make for the 1970s because of the effects of other influences on Canadian trade, including two serious recessions in the United States, one of which was not shared in Canada, and the decision by the Canadian government to restrict severely exports of oil and natural gas to the United States. In addition, most other major industrialized countries have maintained floating exchange rates since early 1973, so comparing the growth of Canadian trade to that of the rest of the world during the mid-1970s would be meaningless. The total volume of Canadian trade (exports plus imports) did grow, however, from Can.$30.6 billion, or 38.3 percent of Canadian GNP in 1970, to Can.$79.7 billion, or 42.0 percent of GNP, in 1976; it therefore seems that the adoption of a flexible exchange rate in 1970 did not hinder Canadian trade.[4]

---

[4] International Monetary Fund, *International Financial Statistics*, various issues, Canadian tables.

CHART 12

Dollar Values of Canadian^a Exports plus Imports Expressed
As Percentages of Total Dollar Values of World^b
Exports plus Imports, 1928-63

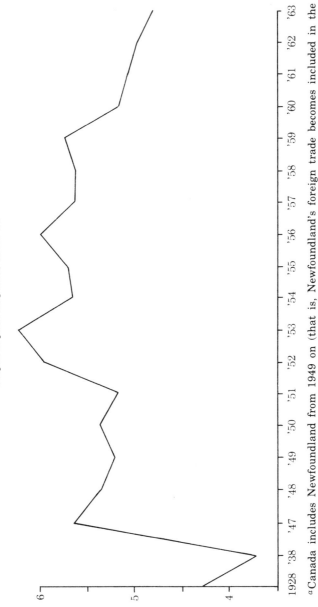

^{a}Canada includes Newfoundland from 1949 on (that is, Newfoundland's foreign trade becomes included in the Canadian figure, but trade between Newfoundland and the rest of Canada becomes domestic rather than international); this complication is of small importance.
^{b}The "world" excludes mainland China, the Soviet Union, and some Eastern European countries.

Source: See Appendix Table A.9.

Investment Impacts

The same conclusion apparently holds true for capital flows. Table 1 in Chapter 3 shows no apparent decline in transactions after 1970 and instead suggests continued growth. A recent econometric attempt to measure the effects of flexible exchange rates on long-term capital flows into Canada produced mixed and inconclusive results. According to an article by Askari, Raymond, and Weil, a given change in the long-term interest-rate differential will produce a somewhat larger immediate flow of long-term funds with fixed than with flexible exchange rates, but the resulting flow will last longer with a flexible exchange rate. It was not possible to conclude from the results that there had been any significant change in the total amount of capital moved in response to relative interest rates.[5] It appears that investors may respond somewhat more slowly to relative interest-rate changes in a world of flexible exchange rates, but it is not clear that they ultimately move less money.

The questionnaire asked whether, in the opinion of the respondents, the adoption of a floating exchange rate for the Canadian dollar in 1970 had discouraged Canadian-U.S. capital flows. Nine of the respondents said there had been no effect; only two said there might be a possible reduction in flows. No respondent said that there had been a clear and noticeable reduction in Canadian-U.S. capital flows; nine were sure that there had been no effect. These nine responses came from both sides of the border and included a number of institutions that are among the most active in Canadian-U.S. financial transactions. If there has been any discouraging effect of flexible exchange rates on flows of capital in or out of Canada, it is so small that hardly anybody has been able to perceive it. It now seems reasonable simply to dismiss the argument that a floating exchange rate provides a significant impediment to trade and financial transactions between Canada and the United States.

The questionnaire also asked whether the adoption of a flexible exchange rate by Canada in 1970 had otherwise affected the way in which financial transactions were carried on between Canada and the United States. Except for the increased use of the forward market and other hedging techniques for short-term capital flows that was discussed earlier, the general response was that there had been very few significant changes in the way capital was moved from one country to the other. There were, however, some insights and observations provided by a few respondents that may be of interest.

---

[5] Hussain Askari, Arthur Raymond, and Gordon Weil, "Long-Term Capital Mobility under Alternative Exchange Systems," *Canadian Journal of Economics*, February, 1977, pp. 69-78.

A number of respondents suggested that most borrowers and lenders on both sides of the border felt strongly that the exchange rate was very likely to remain within the 90-110¢ range and that it would probably move within an even narrower margin. This means that Canadian long-term borrowers of U.S. dollars can safely ignore exchange risk as long as U.S. bond yields are at least one percent lower than those prevailing in Canada. If, for example, a Canadian enterprise borrows in U.S. dollars for fifteen years when the exchange rate is Can.$1.00 = U.S.$1.00, the Canadian dollar would have to fall well below U.S.90¢ by the maturity of the bonds for the borrower to lose money if the interest-rate differential is one percent or more. The presumption that the Canadian dollar could not possibly go below U.S.90¢, which turned out to be wrong, meant that Canadian long-term borrowers felt safe selling U.S.-dollar bonds as long as a significant yield differential existed. Canadian borrowers would obviously prefer that the Canadian dollar stay close to U.S.$1.00 so that they can get the full benefit of lower U.S. interest rates, but even a 10 percent depreciation over a ten- or fifteen-year maturity would not be too damaging if it were offset by a one percent annual interest-rate saving.

The assumption that the Canadian dollar would not move radically away from parity with the U.S. dollar has meant that many, or perhaps most, Canadians who borrow long-term funds in the United States do not worry a great deal about exchange-rate risks and hence do relatively little to minimize that risk. U.S.-dollar sinking funds have not been common, although a few respondents said that some of the newer Canadian bond issues in New York included provisions for such sinking funds to reduce exchange risk. It would be interesting to know whether Canadian attitudes toward long-term exchange-rate risks have been affected by the fairly sharp decline of the Canadian dollar to about U.S.88¢ in early 1978. Canadian long-term borrowers who have U.S.-dollar liabilities outstanding have taken large capital losses in the past eighteen months, which would lead one to expect greater attempts to hedge exchange risks in the future.

Recognition of Exchange-Rate Risks

A number of respondents commented on the quite different levels of sophistication about exchange risks found among various Canadian borrowers. Large Canadian corporations and the governments and hydro authorities of Quebec and Ontario were reported to be aware of, and very careful about, the risks inherent in borrowing U.S. funds for conversion into Canadian dollars. They reportedly try to time their new issues for periods when the Canadian dollar is relatively weak and occasionally use the forward market to protect themselves from the effects on the market of announcements of large U.S. borrowings. If Hydro-Québec, for example, is negotiating a large bond placement in New York, forward Canadian dollars may be purchased before the placement is announced to provide a safe route into Canada for the funds. If this were not done, the announcement of the large borrowing might push the Canadian dollar up enough to impose sizable losses on Canadian borrowers when the funds were brought through the exchange market. If a sufficient volume of forward contracts is arranged at a variety of maturities before the issue is completed and announced, Hydro-Québec can merely take delivery of the U.S. dollars and hold short-term U.S.-dollar assets until the forwards mature. The savings may involve much less than a penny on the dollar, but for issues of a few hundred million dollars, even one-tenth of a cent is more than worth very careful planning.

The smaller provinces and municipal borrowers are reportedly unaware of, and uninterested in, these risks and problems. A number of Canadian public sector borrowers are reportedly interested only in the availability of funds and the simple interest rate. They either do not understand or do not care that the total cost of the loan over its maturity can be affected very significantly by the exchange rate at which they bring the funds into Canada and by the rate at which interest payments and the eventual repayment of the capital are made. A number of participants in the markets were surprised by the contrast between the sophistication and planning of Canadian private firms and of the two largest Canadian public borrowers of U.S. funds, on the one hand, and by the lack of such understanding of exchange risks exhibited by the rest of the provinces and by municipalities, on the other hand. One city school system reportedly borrowed short-term DMs in Frankfurt at what appeared to be an attractive interest rate and switched the funds into Canadian dollars to finance school construction without making any attempt to hedge the resulting risks. The DM evidently appreciated by enough over the period of the loan to impose an actual interest rate in excess of 25 percent on the school board.

Despite the unhappy experience of that school system, most Canadian businesses are reportedly very aware of the vastly increased risks arising from exchange exposure in European currencies. As noted earlier, the exchange crises of 1971 and 1973 came as decided shocks to most Canadians, and the sharp movements in the exchange rates for many European currencies have left a strong impression on Canadian businessmen, one reported effect of which is that Canadian firms are very reluctant to invoice foreign-trade transactions in any currency other than Canadian or U.S. dollars. They seem to find forward cover difficult or impossible to arrange in many currencies other than U.S. dollars and are very aware of the possibilities for sizable exchange-rate changes over periods as short as thirty or ninety days. The apparent result is an increased use of the U.S. dollar as the transactions currency for Canadian trade with Europe and Japan. Foreign firms can readily arrange forward cover between their currencies and the U.S. dollar, and Canadian firms can also hedge short-term U.S.-dollar risks easily. It is therefore reportedly easier to arrange Canadian transactions with European or Japanese firms in U.S. dollars than in either Canadian dollars or in another currency. In the era of fixed exchange rates, Canadian firms did not worry about exchange risks on the yen or the DM and were willing to accept exposure for thirty or ninety days, but since 1973 the risks have become too obvious to ignore. This results in much more widespread attempts to cover exchange risks on these transactions, and the U.S. dollar appears to be a convenient transactions currency for that purpose.

Finally, it should be noted that the behavior of traders and investors in Canadian-U.S. transactions is based in part on the unusually deep, resilient, and stable exchange market for the two currencies. Canadian-U.S. merchandise trade constitutes the largest single bilateral trade flow in the world, and the volume of other transactions between the two countries is huge. The result is that the Canadian-dollar/U.S.-dollar exchange market is currently one of the world's largest bilateral exchange markets. In addition, the political and economic climates of the two countries are similar and are more stable than those prevailing in Europe. Whatever the problems facing the governments of the two countries, they are modest compared to those facing Europe. The result is that the Canadian-dollar/U.S.-dollar exchange market is inherently far more stable than almost any other. The volume across the market is huge, and speculative reactions tend to be stabilizing.

Rightly or wrongly, people have much more confidence in the stability of the Canadian-dollar/U.S.-dollar exchange rate than in almost any other exchange rate one could name. This means that the conclusions of a study of the Canadian-U.S. financial relationship under flexible exchange rates may not be fully transferable to other countries and situations. To the extent that other exchange markets are smaller, less resilient, and — more important — less stable than the market for Canadian dollars, the adoption of a flexible exchange rate by other countries might be expected to produce more disruption of normal trade and of financial relationships than has occurred in the Canadian-U.S. case.

The Impact of a Flexible Exchange Rate on Canadian Macro-Economic Policies

The theoretical discussion in Chapter 2 included a brief coverage of the relationship between the adoption of a flexible exchange rate and the management of a country's macro-economic policies, the main point of which was that the adoption of a flexible exchange rate greatly increases both the independence and the effectiveness of domestic monetary policy. With a combination of a fixed exchange rate and internationally integrated capital markets, Canada's monetary policy is largely determined by the U.S. Federal Reserve System. With a flexible exchange rate, however, the Bank of Canada has far more freedom to determine its own policies and far more reason to expect these policies to be effective.

The purpose of the following discussion is to evaluate whether Canada's experience with a flexible exchange rate supports this theory. As noted earlier, Canada had a flexible exchange rate from 1950 to 1962 and, after a period in which the rate was pegged at U.S.92.5¢, returned to a float in June, 1970. As a result of this long and unique history with a flexible exchange rate, Canada's experience has attracted a great deal of research attention. The combination of good statistics and a long period without a parity has made the Canadian international sector one of the most heavily studied and analyzed among the industrialized countries. (Baseball has sometimes been described as an island of activity surrounded by statistics; Canada occasionally appears to be an island of statistics surrounded by econometricians.)

The advent of large, disaggregated econometric models has made it possible to run simulations of the behavior of the Canadian and other economies to estimate how they would respond to a particular policy change or external shock. To the degree that the models accurately represent the structure of an economy, such simulations represent an approximation of the type of "control experiment" that has previously been possible in the natural sciences but not in the social sciences. Until these models became available, it was not possible to estimate with any accuracy how the Canadian economy would behave during a particular period of time if only one critical variable or policy were changed, since it is obviously impossible to repeat the period with the desired change.

Large, disaggregated models of the Canadian economy now make it possible, however, to approximate such a repetition of history. The model is run through the period with the desired change in one policy or variable, and the results suggest how the economy would have responded to this circumstance. The validity of the results of such simulations depends critically, however, on the extent to which the econometric model in use accurately represents the basic structure of the economy — and such models are far from perfect. They do, however, represent a vast improvement over previously available techniques for estimating (or guessing) how an economy would respond to a particular policy change. Simulations with such models are not precisely analogous to a control experiment in biology or chemistry, since the "experiment" is run with an abstract, and hence somewhat unrealistic, model of the economy rather than with the economy itself, but they can be viewed as an approximation of such a control experiment.

Disaggregated econometric models of the Canadian economy have existed since the early 1960s, with continued improvements and further disaggregation occurring since then. One of the most popular uses of these models has been to run simulations of the Canadian economy that compare its response to a particular event or policy change under fixed and flexible exchange rates. A review of all the literature would require far more time and space than are available, and the results of these studies are so similar that it is not clear that such an effort would produce much additional information. Therefore, this discussion will emphasize a few of the better-known and more recent studies. The emphasis on more recent simulations is based on the presumption that the quality and the accuracy of the available econometric models have improved considerably in recent years, so that the newest studies are likely to be the most dependable. It must be kept in mind, however, that even the largest and most current econometric models represent a vast oversimplification of the underlying economy and are consequently less than fully reliable. The more disaggregated and more recent models, however, probably do suggest approximately how the Canadian economy would respond to a particular policy shift under different exchange-rate regimes.

Monetary-Policy Effectiveness

The available econometric studies virtually all support the theoretical conclusion that Canadian monetary policy has been both far more independent and more effective under a flexible than under a fixed exchange rate. John Helliwell and John Lester recently used RDXII, a large econometric model developed by the Bank of Canada, to simulate the response of the Canadian economy to a shift in monetary policy under various exchange-rate regimes. These simulations indicated that monetary-policy shifts had approximately twice the effect on GNP with flexible exchange rates as with the previous pegged, or "Bretton Woods," exchange-rate system. When the exchange rate was made even more rigid than it had been under Bretton Woods (which allowed a narrow band of one percent plus or minus around a parity), monetary policy became even less effective. In one simulation with a rigidly fixed exchange rate, over 90 percent of the change in the domestic money supply caused by a monetary-policy shift was neutralized by capital flows and their effects on the Canadian balance of payments. The Helliwell and Lester simulations reached the strong and unambiguous conclusion that the impact of Canadian monetary policy on GNP was greatly enhanced by exchange-rate flexibility.[6]

---

[6] John Helliwell and John V. Lester, "External Linkages of the Canadian Monetary

J. L. Carr, G. V. Jump, and J. A. Sawyer reached the same conclusion using the TRACE econometric model of the Canadian economy.[7] Monetary policy has only modest effects on GNP when the Canadian dollar is pegged but gains considerable impact if the exchange rate is allowed to float. In these simulations, a 5 percent addition to the Canadian money supply adds over $600 million to Canadian GNP with a flexible exchange rate but only $118-237 million (depending on assumptions about sterilization policies) with a fixed exchange rate. Variations between the structures of the RDXII and TRACE models mean that slightly different numbers emerge from the two sets of simulations, but the same general conclusion holds in both cases.

Similar results are found in earlier work by Caves and Reuber, based on simulations using an econometric model developed by Lawrence Officer, and in a still earlier article by Rudolph Rhomberg.[8] These efforts were designed to compare the effectiveness of Canadian monetary policy under alternative exchange-rate regimes; although a number of quite different econometric models were used, the results were similar. The recent history of the Canadian economy strongly indicates that monetary policy is a far more effective domestic macro-economic tool if Canada maintains a flexible or floating exchange rate. The combination of a fixed exchange rate and the extensive integration of the capital markets of Canada and the United States meant that Canadian monetary policy was largely determined in Washington and that attempts by the Bank of Canada to adopt a different policy were doomed to be frustrated.

Business-Cycle Linkage

The Carr, Jump, and Sawyer simulations also indicated that a flexible exchange rate gives Canada a considerable degree of automatic protection from U.S. business cycles. With a fixed exchange rate a U.S. recession quickly produces a sharp decline in the demand for Canadian exports, a balance-of-trade deficit, and a resulting Canadian recession. The fixed parity means that the decline in U.S. demand is translated directly into a net reduction in the demand for Canadian goods and hence into a parallel downturn in the Canadian economy. With a flexible exchange rate, however, the reduction in

---

System," *Canadian Journal of Economics*, November, 1976, pp. 646-67.

[7] J. L. Carr, G. V. Jump, and J. A. Sawyer, "The Operation of the Canadian Economy under Fixed and Flexible Exchange Rates: Simulation Results from the TRACE Model," *Canadian Journal of Economics*, February, 1976, pp. 102-20.

[8] Richard Caves and Grant Reuber, *Canadian Economic Policy and the Impact of International Capital Flows* (Toronto: Private Planning Association of Canada and the University of Toronto Press, 1969), pp. 55-66; Lawrence H. Officer, *An Econometric Model of the Canadian Economy under Fluctuating Exchange Rates* (Cambridge, Mass.: Harvard University Press, 1968); Rudolph Rhomberg, "A Model of the Canadian Economy under Fixed and Flexible Exchange Rates," *Journal of Political Economy*, February, 1964, pp. 22-24.

the U.S. demand for Canadian goods produces a decline in the demand for Canadian dollars to pay for these goods and a resulting depreciation of the Canadian dollar. This decline in the Canadian dollar causes a recovery of the Canadian trade balance, largely protecting the Canadian economy from the aggregate demand effects of the U.S. downturn. The Carr, Jump, and Sawyer simulations indicated that a recession in the United States would have between seven and ten times the impact on the Canadian economy under a fixed exchange rate as under a float. One year of no economic growth in the United States would cost Canada between $780 million and $1,059 million in lost output under a fixed parity, but only $101 million under a floating exchange rate.[9]

Fiscal-Policy Effectiveness

The conclusion to be reached from the recent simulations is that Canadian fiscal policy is more effective with a flexible than with a fixed exchange rate. This conclusion suggests the dominance of the trade-account effects over the capital-account effects of a fiscal-policy shift. As was noted in Chapter 2, work by Robert Mundell and others has suggested that an expansionary fiscal policy should produce an increase in economic activity that would be paralleled by an increase in the demand for money.[10] If the central bank does not allow the money supply to grow, interest rates will increase, attracting capital inflows. With a flexible exchange rate, the result will be an appreciation of the local currency, which will reduce the trade balance and hence the level of domestic aggregate demand. As a result, a floating exchange rate is supposed to reduce significantly the effectiveness of fiscal policy unless the central bank cooperates by adjusting the money supply to avoid changes in interest rates. The expectation that Canadian fiscal policy would be more effective with a fixed than with a flexible exchange rate was supported by some earlier econometric work, including the Caves and Reuber volume and the Rhomberg simulations.[11]

As argued in Chapter 2, the opposite conclusion can be reached if it is assumed that the trade-account effects of an increase in domestic economic activity are larger than the capital-account effects. An expansionary fiscal policy, for example, would increase economic activity, which would in turn increase the domestic demand for imports. With a fixed exchange rate, this increase in imports produces a trade deficit, which is contractionary and reduces the impact of the fiscal expansion. With a flexible exchange rate, however, the increase in import demand causes a depreciation of the local currency, which keeps the trade account from deteriorating,

---

[9] Carr, Jump, and Sawyer, *op. cit.*, p. 17.
[10] Robert A. Mundell, "Flexible Exchange Rates and Employment Policy," *Canadian Journal of Economics and Political Science*, November, 1961, pp. 509-17.
[11] Caves and Reuber, *op. cit.*, and Officer, *op. cit.*

thereby greatly reducing the contractionary effect. The conclusion as to which effect is stronger depends to a great extent on whether the degree of integration of capital markets is greater than the integration of goods markets. A flexible exchange rate reduces the effectiveness of fiscal policy if capital markets are closely integrated and goods markets are not. In this instance the capital inflows created by rising interest rates will be greater than the increase in imports caused by growing incomes in the case of an expansionary fiscal policy, and the local currency will appreciate. If goods markets are closely integrated and capital flows are less sensitive to modest shifts in the domestic demand for money, however, the increase in imports caused by an expansionary fiscal policy will exceed the capital inflows caused by interest-rate increases, and the local currency will depreciate. This would enhance the effectiveness of the expansionary fiscal policy.

Although past econometric work has tended to support the view that a flexible exchange rate has reduced the effectiveness of Canadian fiscal policy, more recent simulations, based on newer and presumably more dependable econometric models of the economy, have reached the opposite conclusion. The Carr, Jump, and Sawyer simulations using the TRACE model dealt with this issue and concluded that the trade-account effects of fiscal-policy shifts dominated the capital-account effects, so that an expansionary fiscal policy produced downward pressure on the Canadian dollar. Under a flexible-exchange-rate regime the resulting depreciation of the Canadian dollar enhanced the effectiveness of the fiscal expansion.[12] Separate simulations by Helliwell with the RDXII model indicated that fiscal policy is equally effective under fixed and flexible exchange rates, while Leipziger constructed his own model and used it to conclude that fiscal policy is slightly stronger with flexible exchange rates.[13] Although the evidence is not as conclusive as that for monetary policy, the most recent research indicates that flexible exchange rates do not significantly weaken, and may even enhance slightly, the effectiveness of Canadian fiscal policy.

Summary

In summary, the clear conclusion of the simulations discussed thus far is that Canada receives major macro-economic policy benefits from the maintenance of a flexible exchange rate. The extensive trade and financial ties between the Canadian and U.S.

---

[12] Carr, Jump, and Sawyer, op. cit., pp. 113-14.
[13] John Helliwell, "Trade, Capital Flows, and Migration As Channels for the International Transmission of Stabilization Policies," in Albert Ando, Richard Herring, and Richard Marston, eds., International Aspects of Stabilization Policies (Boston: Boston Federal Reserve Bank, 1974), pp. 244-45; Danny Leipziger, "Capital Movements and Economic Policy: Canada under a Flexible Rate," Canadian Journal of Economics, February, 1974, pp. 59-74.

economies mean that a fixed exchange rate ties Canada rigidly to U.S. business cycles and to U.S. monetary policy. Under these circumstances the macro aspects of the Canadian economy come close to being merely an extension of those in the United States. A flexible exchange rate greatly reduces the strength of this linkage. Canada's tendency automatically to import U.S. business cycles is considerably reduced, and the independence and effectiveness of Canadian monetary policy in dealing with whatever cyclical problems do develop is greatly enhanced. Although the results of the simulations are less dramatic in the case of fiscal policy, it appears that little or nothing is lost by the adoption of a flexible exchange rate, and it is quite possible that fiscal-policy shifts also become more effective in this environment.

Practical Limitations on Exchange-Rate Flexibility

The conclusion that a floating exchange rate makes Canada both more independent of the United States and more effective in managing aggregate demand assumes that the Canadian government is actually prepared to allow the exchange rate to move freely in response to major policy shifts. If large and sudden exchange-rate shifts can be expected from monetary-policy shifts, however, potentially serious problems arise, raising questions about the feasibility of such policy changes. As noted in Chapter 2, large exchange-rate changes have highly disruptive effects on a relatively open economy and are consequently likely to be politically unpopular. Depreciation of the Canadian dollar is inflationary, tends to increase profits in traded-goods industries at the expense of other incomes, and imposes capital losses on Canadians with liabilities denominated in U.S. dollars. None of these effects are likely to be popular, particularly since so many Canadian enterprises and government units have large, unhedged U.S.-dollar liabilities. Although an appreciation of the Canadian dollar has the opposite effect and would therefore seem to be popular, it produces other repercussions that are almost equally troublesome. Most critically, an appreciation of the Canadian dollar significantly cuts the profits and market opportunities for Canadian exporting and import-competing industries and consequently reduces domestic aggregate demand. In Canada a large number of very important industries would be injured. To the extent that major export industries are concentrated in areas such as British Columbia, serious local recessions can result.[14]

There is therefore an understandable tendency in Ottawa to try to avoid sudden and large exchange-rate changes in either direction. This has meant that Canadian monetary policy is not quite as independent as theory would suggest. During 1971 the Bank of Canada

---

[14] Robert M. Dunn, Jr., "Exchange Rate Rigidity, Investment Distortions, and the Failure of Bretton Woods," *Princeton Essays in International Finance* 97 (February, 1973).

apparently ran a somewhat more expansionary monetary policy than it would have preferred for purely domestic purposes in order to avoid a further appreciation of the Canadian dollar, which would have produced additional injury to major export industries. The depreciation of the Canadian dollar in early 1978 was unpopular for other reasons, and it may be that the Bank of Canada did not allow interest rates to fall quite as rapidly as it might otherwise choose in order to avoid a further decline in the exchange rate. As noted earlier, the Canadian dollar's decline from about U.S.$1.03 in mid-1976 to about U.S.89¢ by mid-1978 increased a wide range of Canadian prices and imposed significant capital losses on Canadians with uncovered U.S.-dollar liabilities.

There are additional psychological, and hence political, effects of a depreciation of the Canadian dollar that are troublesome. Such an exchange-rate change is widely seen as a "weakening" of the currency and hence as a judgment by the market that an economy is competitively weak. This is not flattering for a country's self-image, as the United States has been discovering. The decline of the Canadian dollar was analyzed in these terms in a number of Canadian newspaper editorials.

> We as a nation are being judged by world money markets to be an unproductive bunch of wasteful complainers, led by a government that can't bite the bullet. The verdict is accurate. *Ottawa Citizen* (August 8, 1977)
>
> Part of our trouble today lies in the simple fact that, thanks to an inflated wage scale, it costs more to produce things in Canada than it does in the U.S. . . . Not until the cost-price structure is brought to a competitive level, and not until the government puts its own financial house in order, can Canadians hope for much relief. *Winnipeg Free Press* (August 13, 1977)
>
> It [the Canadian dollar] is losing its value because the rest of the world doubts the Trudeau government's ability to run Canada's economy properly. . . . The problem has been, all along, the Trudeau government's unwillingness to deal seriously with the country's economic problems. The decline in the dollar shows that the rest of the world has come to the same conclusion. *Toronto Star* (August 5, 1977)

Although these editorials vastly oversimplify the reasons for the exchange-rate movement, they do indicate some of the psychological and political implications of a sizable depreciation of a currency. As a result, the Canadian government is unlikely to run fiscal policy, or allow the Bank of Canada to determine monetary policy, without reference to likely effects on the exchange market. Although Canadian fiscal and monetary policies gain a considerable degree of independence and additional effectiveness under a flexible exchange rate, that independence is hardly absolute. As long as large exchange-rate changes have widespread and disruptive effects throughout the Canadian economy, with resulting political implications, fiscal and monetary policies are almost certain to be affected by a desire to maintain some stability in the exchange market.

Although a floating exchange rate does not make it possible for a government or a central bank to ignore the international sector of the economy in determining macro-economic policies, such a system still provides far more independence from balance of payments constraints than that existing with a fixed parity. Despite the restraints provided by the necessary goal of avoiding large and disruptive exchange-rate changes, the Bank of Canada is not tied to the U.S. Federal Reserve System under the current exchange-rate regime, as it clearly was between 1962 and 1970.

Conclusions

Since Canadian demand-management policies are both more independent and more effective with a flexible exchange rate and since there is no evidence that the volume of foreign trade or of capital flows has been significantly affected by the absence of a parity, the net benefits to Canada of a floating exchange rate seem clear. There has been some fear expressed in academic circles and elsewhere that the macro-economic-policy benefits of a floating exchange rate would be largely or wholly offset by costs in the form of a reduced volume of international trade and of capital flows caused by the additional risks and uncertainty associated with flexible exchange rates. There is no convincing, or even unconvincing, evidence of any measurable — to say nothing of significant — reduction in the volume of international transactions since Canada abandoned a parity in 1970. The evidence suggests the same conclusion for Canada's 1950-62 experience. Flexible exchange rates are obviously not without difficulties, and the current float is clearly somewhat managed, or "dirty," but Canada's experience does provide strong support for remaining with the current system rather than returning to a parity. At least for Canada, the long debate between the proponents of fixed versus flexible exchange rates seems to be settled. In this case the proponents of fixed exchange rates lost — and they lost overwhelmingly.

In fairness, it should be noted again that a number of circumstances make it particularly likely that Canada would have a more successful experience with the flexible exchange rate than would many other countries. As a result, the favorable conclusions of this analysis of Canada's flexible-exchange-rate experiment may not be directly or fully applicable elsewhere. The massive volume of trade and capital flows between Canada and the United States produces a deeper, more resilient, and more efficient exchange market than could be expected in most other countries. The 1950-62 Canadian history of a floating exchange rate means that this is not a new system that bankers, exporters and importers, and government agencies must learn about as they carry on their activities. The learning process for Canada was already well-advanced by the end of the 1950s. Finally, whatever the current difficulties of the Trudeau administration, the political climate is more stable in Canada than in most other industrialized countries. Participants in the exchange market have more knowledge about, and confidence in, Canada's economic policies than is typical elsewhere. This makes for stable expectations and therefore for a relatively stable exchange market.

Although the Canadian context provides an unusually favorable climate for a flexible exchange rate, this regime has also worked better than had been expected (or feared) in most other industrialized countries. Although Canada may provide the strongest case against fixed parities, the general experience of the industrialized countries during the 1973-77 period hardly suggests a return to the Bretton Woods system. It appears certain that most industrialized countries will remain without fixed parities for the time being, and the particularly successful Canadian experience with flexible exchange rates may be an object lesson encouraging this result.

5

Conclusions: Policy Issues and Options

The previous chapters have anlayzed both the theory of international financial integration and the recent experience of Canada and the United States with integration of their capital markets. The purpose of this concluding chapter is to discuss some of the policy issues raised by the relationship between Canadian and U.S. capital markets and the policy options facing the Canadian government in dealing with these issues.

Although the widely discussed "Third Option" (under which the Canadian government decided in 1972 to reduce the extent to which the Canadian economy is dependent on that of the United States) no longer retains the apparent importance in Ottawa that it had a few years ago, a dominant long-term issue in Canadian international economic policy will always be just how closely the real and the financial sectors of the Canadian economy should be integrated with those of the United States.[1] Canada's current domestic difficulties have temporarily diverted the attention of policy-makers in Ottawa and of the public at large from this issue, but this diversion is likely to end as soon as the problem in Quebec and in the domestic economy have been resolved. Whether it is called the Third Option or some other name, the question of the degree to which Canada, and particularly the Canadian economy, ought to be connected to the United States will ultimately remain a major issue in the country.

---

[1] Mitchell Sharp, "Canada-U.S. Relations: Options for the Future," *International Perspectives*, Autumn, 1972, pp. 1-24. In this landmark article, written while Mr. Sharp was the Canadian Minister of External Affairs, the government announced its intention to move away from Canada's historic level of integration with, and dependence on, the United States. This policy became widely known as the Third Option, and it was to be pursued both by making the Canadian economy stronger and more independent and by actively cultivating Canada's relations with foreign countries other than the United States. This policy was widely viewed in the United States as being at least slightly anti-American, but the Canadian government argued that it was instead merely pro-independence and supportive of more diversified foreign ties. Because of Canada's current internal problems and its lack of notable concrete successes in cultivating ties with other countries, very little is now heard of the Third Option, although this may change as some of Canada's difficulties are resolved.

Policies to Reduce Canada's Need for Foreign Capital

In the context of this volume, Canada's dependence on net inflows of foreign capital in general, and on U.S. capital in particular, represents the most important single aspect of the broader question of Canada's independence of the United States. If Canada does intend to become more independent of, and hence less closely tied to, its neighbor, a major policy goal must be the reduction of Canada's need for continuing net inflows of capital. The advanced state of Canada's economic development might lead to the expectation that Canada would have long since ceased to be a net importer of capital and would instead be a net lender to the rest of the world. The high capital intensity of the Canadian economy's leading sectors; a history of heavy immigration of young adults, which has required particularly rapid economic growth to avoid excessive unemployment; and Canadian policies that have constrained the overall rate of domestic savings have, however, all combined to keep Canada dependent on large net capital inflows.

The nature of Canada's resource base and the resulting pattern of comparative advantage make it unlikely that major changes can or should be adopted with respect to the first of these three factors. Canadian long-term prosperity will continue to be enhanced by growth in natural-resource-based industries (which are inherently capital-intensive), particularly in a world in which such resources are increasingly scarce and therefore expensive. It would be unwise for Canada to reduce required levels of investment by moving the economy away from its pattern of comparative advantage, particularly when one can foresee increasingly attractive terms of trade for resource-based economies.

The other two factors that have made Canada dependent on continuing net inflows of capital can, however, be changed. Canada could pursue policies that would reduce the rate of growth of the labor force, and thus the rate of economic growth required to maintain full employment. Ottawa could also adopt policies that would increase the total level of savings generated by the economy at any given level of GNP and the proportion of the economy's investment that would be financed domestically. If appropriate policies were adopted in both areas, Canada could turn its chronic current-account deficit into at least a rough equilibrium, and perhaps into a surplus, over a period of a few years. A permanent equilibrium in Canada's current account would represent an end to that country's reliance on net capital inflows, and a current-account surplus would produce a reduction in Canada's net indebtedness to the rest of the world, and to the United States in particular. The policies necessary to end Canada's need for foreign capital are not easy to formulate and may not be politically popular. They are, however, feasible; and if Canada is serious about becoming a more independent economy, they ought to be considered.

The rate of growth of the Canadian labor force could be reduced through a continuation of the recent tightening of Canada's immigration policies. The data presented in Chapter 3 make it clear that a large proportion of the past growth of Canada's labor force was the direct result of immigration. A significant reduction in rates of immigration would produce a decline in the level of plant and equipment investment and in the rate of economic growth required to keep Canada at, or close to, full employment. Such a reduction in the necessary rates of investment and of economic growth in Canada would make it far easier to finance domestic investment from domestic savings.

The rapid rate of growth of the labor force is only one of the reasons for Canada's dependence on foreign capital. Low rates of total domestic savings represent an equally important factor but are also subject to change through government policies. As discussed in Chapter 3, a sizable part of the private sector's savings have been absorbed by public sector deficits, leaving insufficient domestic funds (and resources) for levels of investment in the private sector necessary for economic growth. This results in relatively high rates of return to capital, which are necessary to attract net inflows of foreign funds. These funds, in turn, have been required to finance chronic current-account deficits.

Current-account deficits provide the real resources necessary for an economy to invest domestically more than it saves. A reduction or elimination of net capital inflows requires an increase in the domestic savings rate, unless economic growth is to suffer, and this in turn necessitates a significant reduction in public sector deficits. If public sector deficits are significantly reduced through tax increases and/or expenditure reductions, the reduced demand for funds in Canadian capital markets will make it far easier to finance private sector investments domestically. The restrictive effect of this tighter fiscal policy can be offset by a modest easing of monetary policy, leaving the level of aggregate demand unchanged. A trade-off of tighter fiscal policy for a more expansionary monetary policy can be designed that will avoid undesirable cyclical effects while shifting domestic resources from consumption (both private and public) to investment. Tighter fiscal policy reduces private and/or public consumption, and easier monetary policy increases domestic investment. At a given level of output and income, the domestic economy consumes less and consequently saves and invests more. The increase in savings and in domestically financed investment would reduce or eliminate Canada's need for net inflows of capital.

This set of policies may seem simple and obvious, but it is politically very difficult. Tax increases and/or public-sector-expenditure reductions are certain to be unpopular. Voters are always in favor of economy in government as an abstract principle, but attempts to reduce specific expenditures result in strenuous opposition. Canadian voters have enjoyed the benefits of public expenditures well in excess of tax payments and will understandably be reluctant to give up these apparently "free" benefits. Unfortunately, the benefits have not been free. The Canadian economy has been able to consume (publicly and privately) and invest more than the economy produces because of an ongoing net inflow of capital from the rest of the world and especially from the United States. This has resulted in the rapid growth of Canada's net debtor position and in the continuing dependence of the Canadian economy on foreign capital. Canada can continue to consume and invest more than its economy produces if it is willing to remain dependent on the United States and on other countries for capital and to allow its net indebtedness position to continue to grow. If Canada is serious about becoming more independent of the United States, however, this pattern will have to be changed. Canada will have to save more and probably invest less. A reduction in the rate of growth of the labor force will produce a modest reduction in the economy's need for plant and equipment investment, but the main emphasis will have to be on increased aggregate domestic savings. This requires a reduction in consumption (private plus public), which in turn requires a significant and permanent reduction in public sector deficits. This will not be easy or popular, but it is a necessary cost of making Canada less dependent on foreign capital — which really means U.S. capital. If Canada wants to make the Third Option meaningful, this is the place to begin.

Canadian-U.S. Financial Intermediation: Policy Options

Canada's use of New York as an intermediary between domestic savers who want to hold short-term assets and borrowers who want long-term funds represents another area in which Ottawa might consider taking actions that would make the economy more independent of the United States. To the extent that Canadian financial institutions carry on more of this intermediary function, flows of short-term funds south and long-term funds back to Canada would decline. This would reduce the degree of integration of the two sets of capital markets, thereby making Canada more independent of the United States. If an increase in this independence remains a basic goal of the Canadian government, various policies might be undertaken to increase the efficiency and the effectiveness of Canadian financial markets in intermediating between the differing needs of Canadian savers and borrowers.

It should be noted at the outset that the purely economic arguments for reducing the integration of the two capital markets and for moving more or all of the intermediation process back to Canada are weak. The difference between U.S. long-term interest rates at which Canadians borrow in New York and the short-term yields at which Canadians lend to New York constitutes the cost to Canada of importing New York's services as a financial intermediary. Canada imports these services for the same reasons that any economy imports any good or service — that is, relative costs. The fact that the U.S. yield curve is typically less steep than that prevailing in Canada means that intermediary services are cheaper in the United States than in Canada. Since the U.S. curve is typically not very steep, the cost to Canada of importing intermediary services is not high. The economic arguments for "protectionism" in the form of capital controls or taxes are no stronger than they are in other markets.

To the extent that a political decision is taken in Canada to make the economy less integrated with, and less dependent on, the United States, however, economic arguments about relative costs may not be dominant, and policies might be adopted to reduce this two-way flow of capital. Capital controls would be a particularly unfortunate method of increasing the role of Canadian financial institutions in the domestic intermediation process, both because they are very inefficient and because they are difficult (or impossible) to enforce. Capital controls produce resource misallocations very similar to those produced by tariffs, and they have the additional disadvantage of virtually inviting dishonesty. There are more ways of moving money into or out of a country than any government official can imagine, and capital controls create an open season for human ingenuity and avarice. Even in the United Kingdom, where obedience to the law has traditionally been a central cultural virtue, long-standing capital controls have created temptations for ingenious capital-market participants. The recent scandal in the Bank of England makes it all too clear that these temptations are not always resisted, and there is no way of knowing how much capital has been moved out of the United Kingdom through transfer pricing and other means.[2] Capital is the most mobile of all resources, and attempts to restrict its movements ultimately do little more than encourage disrespect for the law.

If Ottawa decides to try reducing the extent to which Canada imports intermediation services from New York, one would hope that it would do so by changing the underlying cost relationships, rather than through inefficient and failure-prone capital controls.

To some extent the natural growth and the maturing of Canadian capital markets will automatically increase the extent to which intermediation is completed locally and will reduce the flows of capital to and from New York. As was suggested in Chapters 2 and 3,

---

[2] An official of the Bank of England was recently convicted of taking part in a conspiracy to violate U.K. exchange rules. Funds were brought into the United Kingdom under a much more favorable exchange rate than the law allowed, and large profits were made on the differential between the exchange rates. The official was convicted of fraudulently certifying the eligibility of these transactions for the more favorable exchange rate.

the steepness of a country's yield curve is in part an inverse function of the maturity, depth, and stability of its financial markets and institutions. The natural trend in Canada ought to be toward a flatter yield curve and thus toward less reliance on foreign intermediaries.

It would be possible, however, for Ottawa to encourage this trend through a number of policy initiatives. First, Canadian domestic financial markets could be made more competitive: legal barriers to entry in various segments of the financial markets could be reduced, and different types of financial institutions could be allowed to compete with each other more directly than has been possible in the past. Increased competition in financial markets will automatically reduce the difference between the short-term interest rates at which Canadian financial institutions borrow and the longer-term yields at which they lend. This will reduce the volume of short-term funds flowing south and of long-term funds returning to Canada. U.S. exports of intermediary services to Canada are partly a competitive response to relatively concentrated financial markets in Canada. To the extent that Canadian markets can be made more competitive, U.S. financial institutions will be less successful in exporting intermediary services to Canada, and the two-directional flows of capital between the two countries will be reduced. This would make Canadian financial markets more independent of the United States.

The same result would be encouraged by changes in financial regulatory policies that cause Canadian banks and other financial institutions to restrict the percentage of their portfolios held in long-term forms. A reduction in secondary-reserve requirements would be one example of such a change. The Bank of Canada and other federal and provincial regulatory authorities might adopt other devices to encourage a shift in financial-institution assets toward longer maturities. One approach might be through tax policies. Earnings on long-term domestic assets held by either institutions or individuals might be given preferable tax treatment, and yields on short-term claims less preferable treatment. This might be too complicated for individual tax returns but should not be too difficult for taxation of financial institutions. A modest change in the relative tax rates on earnings from long-term and short-term assets could produce a significant shift in relative asset preferences. As the portfolios of major financial institutions were shifted toward longer average maturities, the Canadian yield curve would become less steep, and the role of New York as an intermediary between Canadian savers and borrowers would be reduced.

Debt-management policy represents another option for flattening the yield curve and reducing the importation of intermediary services. If the Canadian public sector would shift its borrowing activities to shorter average maturities, the results would be a significant reduction in the relative demand for long-term funds, a flatter yield curve, and less money flowing back and forth to New York.

The public sector is a dominant borrower in Canada, and its activities have an important effect on relative yields. Although Ottawa has recently been borrowing at shorter maturities, the provincial governments and their agencies continue to borrow long-term funds heavily; if this borrowing were shifted to somewhat shorter maturities, the ability of the rest of the economy to find long-term funds in Canada would be increased, and there would be less long-term borrowing in New York.

None of these policies alone would produce a major change in the past pattern of financial intermediation, in which short-term funds flow south and return in long-term form, but the adoption of all of them as a package should have a significant effect. A combination of policies designed to increase the competitiveness of financial markets, of regulatory and tax policies designed to shift the assets of financial institutions toward longer maturities, and of provincial debt-management policies that would reduce long-term borrowing by the public sector should flatten the Canadian yield curve and significantly reduce Canadian use of New York markets as financial intermediaries.

Exchange-Rate Policy

Canada's decision in 1970 to abandon a fixed parity was based in large part on its desire to make the economy more independent of cyclical instability and of macro policy changes in the United States. For reasons discussed in Chapters 2 and 4, Canada has little or no macro-economic independence if it maintains a fixed exchange rate and if its capital and goods markets are closely integrated with those of the United States. The adoption of a floating exchange rate greatly weakens the linkage between the business cycles of the two countries and increases both the independence and the effectiveness of Canadian macro-economic policies in dealing with domestic cycles. As a result, Canada's adoption in 1970 of a flexible exchange rate can be seen as a major movement toward reduced economic dependence on the United States.

Until very recently it would have been hard to imagine a serious argument in favor of a return by Canada to a fixed exchange rate. Canada's experience with a fixed rate in the late 1960s was not a happy one. On the other hand, during the 1950s and early 1970s Canada had very successful experiences with a flexible exchange rate.[3] This history would appear to discourage any real consideration of alternative exchange-rate regimes. Between the fall of 1976 and mid-1978, however, the Canadian dollar depreciated from U.S.$1.03

---

[3] For a discussion of Canada's difficulties with a fixed parity during the late 1960s, see Robert M. Dunn, Jr., *Canada's Experience with Fixed and Flexible Exchange Rates in a North American Capital Market* (Montreal and Washington: Canadian-American Committee, 1971), Chaps. 2 and 3.

to less than U.S.90¢. Such a rapid and extreme decline in an exchange rate causes a variety of internal dislocations, as suggested in Chapter 4. This experience has again raised the question of whether a flexible exchange rate is inherently unstable. Some Canadians may be led to conclude that a return to a fixed parity, or at least to the adoption of a crawling peg or a parity with a wide band, would now be advisable.

It seems clear that this would be a particularly unfortunate time to adopt a parity for the Canadian dollar and that Canada was probably very fortunate that it did not have to defend a parity over the period from late 1976 to mid-1978. Canada's cost competitiveness had been deteriorating in many industries as a result of rapid wage increases in relation to labor-productivity growth, and the exchange rate had been supported in 1975-76 primarily by large capital inflows resulting from Canadian bond flotations in New York. The Quebec election undoubtedly shook market confidence, but a sizable slowdown in the scheduling of new Canadian bond issues in the United States during 1977 was at least as important a factor in the decline of the exchange rate. The reduction in long-term capital inflows allowed the exchange market to be largely dominated by the effects of Canada's declining cost competitiveness and of the Quebec election. The resulting decline in the exchange rate, from U.S.$1.03 to U.S.89¢, may have been greater than was necessitated by underlying economic forces, and a modest recovery might be anticipated. When the Quebec issue has been resolved, or at least has become less pressing, and as the somewhat less inflationary budget policies of the public sector have their effects, the market for the Canadian dollar ought to strengthen.

A retreat from flexible exchange rates to a fixed parity under present unsettled market conditions would be seen as a sign of weakness, if not of panic, by the market and would encourage further speculative pressure against the Canadian dollar. Canada adopted a fixed exchange rate in 1962 under similarly unsettled circumstances, resulting in a speculative rush out of Canadian funds. Since Canada currently has less than $5 billion in foreign-exchange reserves — about one month's imports — a major speculative run on the currency would almost certainly overwhelm any new parity. The 1962 experience resulted in an inappropriate exchange rate as well as in a speculative run on the currency; this hardly seems an experience one would want to repeat. If, instead, Ottawa waits for the Quebec situation to be resolved and continues its attempts to restrict excessively rapid rates of growth of the money supply and excessive deficits in the public sector, confidence in the currency will recover, and the exchange rate will reflect that confidence.

When the current difficulties pass, and as a more stable political and economic climate returns, a fixed parity might be made to work, but there will be little or no reason to adopt one. Under those circumstances the flexible exchange rate should return to its previous stability, and arguments for a return to a parity will quickly fade. The recent depreciation of the Canadian dollar is not the cause of Canada's economic problems. It is, instead, the result of a recent history of highly inflationary macro-economic policies, a decline in Canadian bond flotations in New York, uncertainty and doubts caused by the program of price and wage controls, and the Quebec situation. As Ottawa's attempts to enforce less inflationary macro-economic policies and to end price and wage controls continue, confidence in the economy and in the currency should return. Even if the Quebec situation remains unsettled for a time, a return to a more stable climate for economic policy will restore stability in the exchange market. The exchange market has reflected difficulties elsewhere in the economy during the past year, not vice versa. To blame the depreciation of the Canadian dollar for Canada's economic problems would be to blame the messenger for the message.

A flexible exchange rate remains critical to Canada's macro-economic independence and ought not to be abandoned merely because of what are basically temporary problems. If the Canadian government's policies are successful in returning the economy to a more stable course, the exchange market will stabilize, and the Canadian dollar will probably regain some of its recent losses. The current situation does not provide an argument for adopting a parity. It instead argues strongly for remaining with the float and for simply waiting for the more stable macro-economic policies coming from Ottawa to have their predictable effect on the Canadian economy and hence on the exchange market.

Appendix A

Tables

TABLE A.1

Canadian Current Account, Including Retained Earnings, 1950-77

Year	(1) Recorded Current Account (mil. Can.$)	(2) Net Retained Earnings (mil. Can.$)	(3) Adjusted Current Account (1) + (2) (mil. Can.$)	(4) Adjusted Current Account As Percentage of Canadian GNP[a]	(5) Adjusted Current Account As Percentage of Total Net Investment[a]	(6) Adjusted Current Account As Percentage of Total Private Net Investment[a]
1950	-334	64	-398	2.22	16.24	20.62
1951	-512	103	-615	2.84	19.24	24.05
1952	+187	213	-26	.11	0.80	1.05
1953	-448	247	-695	2.69	18.79	23.83
1954	-424	218	-642	2.48	24.87	37.57
1955	-687	269	-956	3.35	28.37	39.47
1956	-1,372	309	-1,681	5.24	32.51	41.74
1957	-1,451	336	-1,787	5.33	38.02	52.98
1958	-1,137	190	-1,327	3.82	32.33	49.02
1959	-1,504	286	-1,790	4.86	38.91	57.89
1960	-1,243	225	-1,468	3.83	35.43	56.83
1961	-982	210	-1,192	3.01	32.88	61.10
1962	-848	261	-1,109	2.58	25.70	45.96
1963	-521	348	-869	1.89	18.82	32.99
1964	-424	461	-885	1.76	15.66	24.40
1965	-1,130	622	-1,752	3.16	22.55	32.88
1966	-1,162	522	-1,684	2.72	18.18	26.22
1967	-449	664	-1,113	1.68	13.74	21.62
1968	-97	692	-789	1.09	9.63	15.15
1969	-917	897	-1,814	2.27	18.74	27.38
1970	+1,106	767	+339	-0.40	-4.08	-6.60
1971	+431	1,098	-667	0.71	6.59	10.47

1972	−386	1,336	−1,722	1.66	14.97	22.85
1973	+96	2,009	−1,913	1.59	12.87	18.11
1974	−1,492	2,533	−4,025	2.78	19.95	27.35
1975	−4,965	2,172	−7,137	4.43	33.28	47.71
1976	−4,329	2,059	−6,388	3.46	25.45	34.45
1977	−4,238	2,285[b]	−6,523	3.14	26.14	36.80
1950-77			−50,628	2.55	20.61	30.01
1950-54			−2,376	2.05	15.64	20.49
1955-59			−7,541	4.55	34.36	48.27
1960-64			−5,523	2.54	24.71	41.82
1965-69			−7,152	2.13	16.63	24.89
1970-77			−28,036	2.41	19.29	27.64
1970-74			−7,988	1.46	12.29	18.02

[a]"Negative" represents current-account surplus (which is a proxy for a capital outflow).
[b]Estimated by author.

Sources: Column 2: T. L. Powrie (with the assistance of M. A. Gormley), *The Contribution of Foreign Capital to Canadian Economic Growth* (Edmonton: Mel Hurtig, 1977), Table A.15. (1977 has been estimated by the author using the Powrie methodology.) Other columns: 1950-71: *Bank of Canada Statistical Summary.* 1972-77: *Bank of Canada Review.*

TABLE A.2

Canadian Public Borrowing, All Currencies, 1950-77
(million Canadian dollars)

Year	(1) Federal Government	(2) Provincial Governments	(3) Municipal Governments	(4) Total
1950	199	159	136	494
1951	−468	250	176	−42
1952	−124	306	152	334
1953	451	272	182	905
1954	−171	293	241	363
1955	535	210	234	979
1956	−766	540	224	−2
1957	−70	547	279	756
1958	1,252	613	348	2,213
1959	723	568	302	1,593
1960	612	486	366	1,464
1961	890	944	333	2,167
1962	801	704	244	1,749
1963	827	897	374	2,098
1964	457	940	401	1,798
1965	−52	759	248	955
1966	430	1,566	349	2,345
1967	900	2,050	466	3,416
1968	1,545	1,944	288	3,777
1969	339	1,953	239	2,531
1970	1,844	2,064	176	3,084
1971	2,547	2,647	323	5,517
1972	1,599	2,969	427	4,995
1973	−147	2,603	399	2,854
1974	4,212	3,774	538	8,524
1975	3,967	6,810	1,221	11,998
1976	4,233	8,204	1,219	13,656
1977	8,024	6,216	1,149	15,389

Sources: 1950-71: *Bank of Canada Statistical Summary.*
1972-77: *Bank of Canada Review.*

TABLE A.3

Role of Immigration in Canadian Labor Force Growth, 1955-77

Year	(1) Civilian Labor Force at End of Period ('000)	(2) Change in Labor Force ('000)	(3) Immigrants Entering Labor Force ('000)	(4) Immigrants Entering Labor Force As Percentage of Change in Labor Force (3) ÷ (2)
1955	5,610	—	—	—
1956	5,782	172	91	52.9
1957	6,008	226	151	66.8
1958	6,137	129	63	48.8
1959	6,242	105	54	51.4
1960	6,411	169	54	32.0
1961	6,521	110	35	31.8
1962	6,615	94	37	39.4
1963	6,748	133	46	34.6
1964	6,933	195	56	28.7
1965	7,141	208	74	35.6
1966	7,420	179	99	55.3
1967	7,694	266	120	45.1
1968	7,919	225	95	42.2
1969	8,162	243	84	34.6
1970	8,374	212	78	36.8
1971	8,631	257	61	23.7
1972	8,920	289	59	20.4
1973	9,322	402	92	22.9
1974	9,706	384	106	27.6
1975	10,060	354	81	22.9
1976	10,308	248	61	24.6
1977	10,753	445	48	10.8

Sources: Statistics Canada, *The Labour Force* (Ottawa, various issues); Manpower and Immigration Canada, *Immigration Statistics* (Ottawa, various issues).

128

TABLE A.4

Trade in Outstanding Securities Between Canada and the United States, 1950-71
(million dollars)

Year	(1) Canadian Sales to United States	(2) Canadian Purchases from United States	(3) Gross Flows (1) + (2)	(4) Net Sales (+) and Purchases (−)
1950	543	289	832	+254
1951	532	542	1,074	−10
1952	448	543	991	−95
1953	385	445	830	−60
1954	619	613	1,232	+6
1955	943	979	1,922	−36
1956	992	948	1,940	+44
1957	735	780	1,515	−45
1958	643	572	1,215	+71
1959	800	740	1,540	+60
1960	655	603	1,258	+52
1961	1,395	1,192	2,587	+203
1962	1,469	1,456	2,925	+13
1963	755	777	1,532	−22
1964	919	960	1,879	−41
1965	1,167	1,390	2,557	−223
1966	1,348	1,859	3,207	−511
1967	2,253	2,595	4,848	−342
1968	3,112	3,477	6,589	−365
1969	2,696	2,609	5,305	+87
1970	1,909	1,982	3,891	−73
1971	2,440	2,297	4,737	+143
Total	26,788	27,648	54,436	−860

Source: Dominion Bureau of Statistics, *Sales and Purchases of Securities Between Canada and Other Countries* (Ottawa: Queen's Printer, 1971), p. 23.

TABLE A.5

**Canadian and U.S. Long- and Short-Term-Yield Spreads,
1956-77**
(percentage points)

Year/Quarter	(1) Canadian Spread	(2) U.S. Spread	(3) Difference
1956: I	1.10	.22	.88
II	.70	.13	.57
III	.33	.20	.13
IV	.48	.21	.27
1957: I	−.05	.32	−.37
II	−.10	.32	−.42
III	.08	.32	−.24
IV	.16	.26	−.10
1958: I	.78	1.07	−.29
II	1.89	2.10	−.21
III	2.32	1.90	.42
IV	2.10	1.04	1.06
1959: I	1.36	.99	.37
II	.43	.85	−.42
III	−.17	1.36	−1.53
IV	.48	0	.48
1960: I	1.26	0	1.26
II	1.82	.63	1.19
III	2.34	1.17	1.17
IV	1.62	1.27	.35
1961: I	1.94	1.46	.48
II	2.08	1.64	.44
III	2.31	1.70	.61
IV	2.27	1.59	.68
1962: I	1.87	1.30	.57
II	1.38	1.24	.14
III	.21	1.16	−.95
IV	1.07	1.14	−.07
1963: I	1.28	1.08	.20
II	1.71	1.08	.63
III	1.50	.75	.75
IV	1.34	.57	.77
1964: I	1.51	.54	.97
II	1.59	.61	.98
III	1.38	.62	.76
IV	1.11	.48	.63
1965: I	1.06	.22	.84
II	.88	.18	.70
III	.69	.25	.44
IV	.22	.22	0
1966: I	.13	−.01	.14
II	.17	−.28	.45
III	.34	−.29	.63
IV	.31	−.38	.69

Year/Quarter	(1) Canadian Spread	(2) U.S. Spread	(3) Difference
1967: I	.63	−.06	.69
II	1.56	.77	.79
III	1.43	.87	.56
IV	1.02	.94	.08
1968: I	.65	.71	−.06
II	.55	.38	.17
III	1.18	.38	.80
IV	1.44	.55	.89
1969: I	1.27	.22	1.05
II	1.13	−.43	1.56
III	.46	−1.17	1.64
IV	.35	−.91	1.26
1970: I	.97	−.47	1.44
II	1.71	.09	1.62
III	1.86	.64	1.22
IV	3.02	1.97	1.05
1971: I	3.39	2.79	.60
II	4.54	2.59	1.95
III	3.80	2.01	1.79
IV	3.38	2.44	.94
1972: I	3.35	3.31	.04
II	3.65	2.83	.82
III	3.40	2.42	.98
IV	2.73	1.94	.79
1973: I	3.07	1.05	2.02
II	1.75	−.06	1.81
III	.20	−2.05	2.25
IV	−.95	−1.20	.25
1974: I	−.01	−.27	.26
II	−1.30	−1.96	.66
III	−.57	−2.37	1.80
IV	.35	.24	.11
1975: I	3.15	2.42	.73
II	3.17	3.49	−.32
III	2.54	2.74	−.20
IV	1.77	3.25	−1.48
1976: I	1.33	3.94	−2.61
II	1.17	3.52	−2.35
III	.97	3.37	−2.40
IV	1.26	3.57	−2.31
1977: I	1.82	3.57	−1.75
II	2.44	3.13	−.69
III	2.21	2.45	−.24
IV	2.15	1.79	+.36

Sources: Canadian short-term yields: *Bank of Canada Statistical Summary*, 1956-71; *Bank of Canada Review*, 1972-77.
U.S. short-term yields: *Federal Reserve Bulletin*, various issues.
Canadian and U.S. long-term yields: various government sources.

TABLE A.6

Performance Comparison of Major Canadian and California Banks, 1970-75

Line	Indicators	Canadian Banks							California Banks						
		1970	1971	1972	1973	1974	1975	Average	1970	1971	1972	1973	1974	1975	Average
1	Gross income as % of assets	7.85	6.82	6.38	6.96	8.85	8.77	7.61	6.56	5.79	5.51	6.39	8.12	7.50	6.65
2	Net income as % of assets	0.38	0.37	0.39	0.36	0.36	0.45	0.39	0.61	0.49	0.46	0.40	0.36	0.42	0.46
3	Net income as % of stockholders' equity	11.43	11.21	12.15	12.12	13.41	16.40	12.79	11.06	10.62	10.63	10.81	10.22	10.30	10.61
4	Staff and other expenses as % of assets	2.49	2.44	2.43	2.25	2.28	2.47	2.39	2.74	2.55	2.43	2.39	3.08	3.03	2.70
5	Number of employees per mil. $ assets	2.11	1.90	1.71	1.49	1.30	1.21	1.62	1.79	1.56	1.37	1.18	1.12	1.15	1.36
6	Number of offices per bil. $ assets	32.5	119.3	104.9	88.2	74.5	66.3	79.6	49.9	42.7	39.5	34.7	33.8	33.9	39.1
7	Income from loans as % of gross income	77.9	77.7	77.9	81.7	84.5	84.0	80.6	72.8	67.7	68.6	72.7	75.0	73.5	71.7
8	Income from securities as % of gross income	13.0	12.9	12.2	9.9	8.8	8.6	10.9	11.9	14.8	13.8	10.2	8.5	10.7	11.7
9	Other operating revenues as % of gross income	9.1	9.4	9.9	8.5	6.7	7.5	8.5	15.3	17.6	17.6	17.2	16.6	15.8	16.7
10	Interest expenses as % of gross income	57.8	53.0	49.8	55.2	65.2	60.0	56.8	42.8	44.3	44.4	54.2	56.1	51.3	48.9
11	Staff expenses as % of gross income	16.9	18.6	18.9	17.4	13.9	15.4	16.9	22.8	24.6	24.4	19.0	16.0	19.4	21.0
12	Other operating expenses as % of gross income	14.7	17.2	19.2	15.0	11.8	12.8	15.1	19.0	19.5	19.6	18.4	21.9	21.0	19.9
13	Income taxes as % of gross income	5.7	5.9	6.0	7.3	5.5	6.6	6.2	6.2	3.1	3.4	1.9	1.5	2.7	3.1
14	Net income as % of gross income	4.9	5.4	6.1	5.1	3.6	5.2	5.1	9.3	8.5	8.3	6.1	4.5	5.6	7.1

Sources: Figures have been computed from the annual reports of the banks used in this study, as listed in the text.

TABLE A.7

U.S.-Dollar Assets and Liabilities in Canadian Chartered Banks, End of Period, 1963-77
(million Canadian dollars)

Year	Assets[a]			Percentage of Total Assets	Liabilities[a]			Percentage of Total Liabilities
	Banks	Other	Total		Banks	Other	Total	
1963	2,383 (1,856[b])	820 (221)	3,204 (2,077)	14.5	708 (129)	2,453 (1,348)	3,161 (1,476)	14.3
1964	3,015 (1,909)	1,027 (187)	4,042 (2,095)	16.9	808 (212)	3,294 (1,580)	4,102 (1,793)	17.2
1965	2,388 (1,664)	1,371 (211)	3,759 (1,875)	14.3	1,077 (128)	2,676 (930)	3,753 (1,058)	14.3
1966	2,567 (1,818)	1,554 (286)	4,121 (2,104)	14.6	1,054 (87)	2,897 (679)	3,951 (767)	14.0
1967	3,309 (2,273)	1,307 (95)	4,616 (2,368)	14.6	1,155 (109)	3,357 (732)	4,512 (842)	14.2
1968	3,961 (2,436)	1,313 (62)	5,274 (2,498)	14.4	1,495 (90)	3,432 (450)	4,926 (540)	13.4
1969	6,070 (3,254)	1,606 (57)	7,677 (3,311)	18.0	2,238 (69)	5,582 (802)	7,820 (871)	18.3
1970	6,959 (3,084)	1,758 (57)	8,717 (3,141)	18.4	3,272 (218)	5,344 (712)	8,616 (930)	18.2
1971	5,989 (2,113)	1,854 (74)	7,843 (2,187)	14.4	3,786 (648)	3,942 (831)	7,728 (1,480)	14.2
1972	6,972 (1,985)	1,830 (67)	8,802 (2,052)	13.9	5,405 (777)	3,981 (915)	9,386 (1,693)	14.8

1973	10,056 (2,529)	2,226 (50)	12,283 (2,579)	15.4	7,821 (894)	5,978 (1,075)	13,800 (1,969)	17.3
1974	11,204 (2,414)	3,683 (73)	14,887 (2,486)	15.3	6,863 (887)	9,124 (2,119)	15,987 (3,006)	16.5
1975	10,785 (1,792)	4,986 (123)	15,771 (1,915)	14.6	6,724 (1,412)	9,644 (2,497)	16,369 (3,909)	15.1
1976	13,240 (2,578)	6,157 (173)	19,397 (2,751)	15.3	8,700 (1,449)	11,757 (2,706)	20,457 (4,155)	16.2
1977	14,524 (2,855)	9,417 (195)	23,941 (3,050)	15.9	11,681 (2,248)	13,441 (3,146)	25,121 (5,394)	16.7

[a]By type of customer.
[b]Figures in parentheses are the amounts held by U.S. customers.

Sources: 1963-71: *Bank of Canada Statistical Summary*.
1972-77: *Bank of Canada Review*.

134

TABLE A.8

Canadian Foreign Exchange Reserves, End of Period, 1961-77

Year	Total (mil.U.S.$)	U.S. Dollars (mil. U.S.$)	U.S. Dollars As Percentage of Total
1961	2,292	1,123	49.0
1962	2,561	1,846	72.0
1963	2,613	1,787	68.4
1964	2,890	1,655	57.3
1965	3,037	1,520	50.0
1966	2,702	1,195	44.2
1967	2,717	1,250	46.2
1968	3,046	1,965	64.5
1969	3,106	1,744	56.1
1970	4,679	3,022	64.6
1971	5,570	4,061	72.9
1972	6,050	4,355	72.0
1973	5,768	3,927	68.1
1974	5,825	3,768	64.7
1975	5,326	3,207	60.2
1976	5,843	3,446	59.0
1977	4,608	2,299	49.9

Sources: 1961-71: *Bank of Canada Statistical Summary.*
1972-77: *Bank of Canada Review.*

TABLE A.9

Dollar Values of Canadian[a] Exports plus Imports Expressed As Percentages
of Total Dollar Values of World[b] Exports plus Imports, 1928-63

Year	Percentage	Year	Percentage
1928	4.26	1955	5.70
1938	3.72	1956	5.99
1947	5.66	1957	5.64
1948	5.36	1958	5.62
1949	5.22	1959	5.74
1950	5.38	1960	5.16
1951	5.17	1961	5.07
1952	5.96	1962	4.91
1953	6.19	1963	4.80
1954	5.68		

[a]Canada includes Newfoundland from 1949 on (that is, Newfoundland's foreign trade becomes included in the Canadian figure, but trade between Newfoundland and the rest of Canada becomes domestic rather than international); this complication is of small importance.
[b]The "world" excludes mainland China, the Soviet Union, and some Eastern European countries.
Source: Leland Yeager, *International Monetary Relations: Theory, History, and Policy*, 2nd ed. (New York: Harper and Row, 1976), p. 255.

Appendix B

North American Financial Integration Questionnaire

Two-Directional Capital Flows

1. Canadian bond yields have typically exceeded Canadian short-term interest rates by more than U.S. bond yields have exceeded U.S. short-term interest rates, but this difference has recently been reduced or at times even reversed. Why, in your opinion, has the yield curve historically been steeper in Canada than in the United States, and why has this relationship recently changed?

Was the past yield-curve relationship the result of differing asset and liability preferences in the two countries (Canadian borrowers wanted longer-term funds and Canadian lenders wanted shorter-term assets than was the case in the United States)?

Was it instead the result of differing regulatory situations in the two countries, or of differences in the cost structures of financial institutions in the two countries?

2. Are there important differences in the structures of yields in the two countries, other than those based on maturity (PE ratios versus bond yields, finance paper versus commercial paper versus treasury bills, and so forth)?

Can any important two-directional capital flows be explained through such yield-structure differences?

3. It has sometimes been argued that U.S. investors buy some types of Canadian assets because they are less aware of the risks than are alternative Canadian investors — that is, that Americans buy risky paper that cannot be sold in Canada because they are not aware of the extent of the risks. Do you think that there is anything to this argument? For example, do you think that it is easier to sell Hydro-Québec bonds in New York than in Toronto because New York lenders are less aware of the separatist sentiment in Quebec than are potential Toronto lenders?

Are there any regulatory reasons for differences in the willingness of banks in the two countries to take risks? That is, do central-bank or other regulations make it harder for banks in one country to make risky loans?

How do overall loan-default rates in U.S. banks compare with those of Canadian banks?

Have U.S. banks had better or worse experiences with loans to Canadian borrowers than with loans to U.S. borrowers?

4.   Are there other regulatory or institutional factors encouraging two-directional capital flows? For example, do insurance companies and other large intermediaries distribute their portfolios among assets in Canada and the United States in rough proportion to the distribution of their liabilities in the two countries? Do Canadian and U.S. financial institutions spread their portfolios among assets in both countries in order to reduce risks — that is, on the assumption that one market will be strong when the other is weak and hence that the variance in the value of the portfolio can be reduced by holding assets in both (or many) countries?

Effects of Flexible Exchange Rates

5.   Has Canada's adoption in 1970 of a floating exchange rate affected the way exchange-rate risks are perceived and handled by those moving capital or carrying on merchandise trade where commercial credit terms of 30-90 days are involved?

Have some capital flows been discouraged by the existence of a floating exchange rate — that is, do investors fail to respond to yield differentials in a floating-exchange-rate situation that would have attracted funds in the fixed-exchange-rate period?

Has the use of the forward market to cover such transactions increased since May, 1970? How broad is the forward market in terms of its ability to handle large flows without major changes in the premium or the discount on the Canadian dollar?

Have buy/sell margins in the forward market increased as a result of the float or because of the relatively unsettled conditions in exchange markets?

6.   How is exchange risk handled on Canadian long-term bond issues in New York when forward cover is not available? Do Canadian sellers of U.S.-dollar bonds make any attempt to protect themselves against a depreciation of the Canadian dollar during the period before maturity?

Are U.S.-dollar sinking funds built up during the period before maturity to avoid having to move a large amount of money into U.S. dollars at a time when the rate may be particularly unfavorable?

Do issuers of such bonds try to time new issues for periods in which the Canadian dollar seems particularly weak?

Has Canada's adoption of a flexible exchange rate changed the way in which Canadian sellers of U.S.-dollar bonds behave with regard to exchange risk? That is, has it discouraged Canadians from selling U.S.-dollar bonds?

7. Has there been any change in the typical pattern of financing ordinary merchandise trade? Has the adoption of a flexible exchange rate had any effect on the currency in which such trade is usually invoiced?

Are Canadian exports and imports both still typically invoiced in U.S. dollars so that the Canadian participant in the transactions takes the exchange risk both for exports and imports where commercial credit terms are involved?

Has the flexible exchange rate led to a shortening of maturities on such commercial credit to minimize such risk — that is, 30 days rather than 60 or 90 days?